NASCAR
A FAST HISTORY

By Greg Fielden
and the Auto Editors of Consumer Guide®

Publications International, Ltd.

Louis Weber, CEO
Publications International, Ltd.
7373 North Cicero Avenue
Lincolnwood, Illinois 60712

ISBN-13: 978-1-4127-1155-5
ISBN-10: 1-4127-1155-X

Manufactured in China.

8 7 6 5 4 3 2 1

Library of Congress Control Number: 2004113592

The editors gratefully acknowledge the cooperation of the following people who supplied photography to help make this book possible:

California Speedway, Jack Cansler, Chicagoland Speedway, Chrysler Photographic, Greg Fielden, Ford Motor Company and Wieck Media Services, Inc., Matt Griffith, Phil Hall, Bryan Hallman, Mike Horne, Indianapolis Motor Speedway, International Speedway Corporation, Don Kelly, Tom Kirkland, Mike Laczynski, Larry McTighe, Motor Sports Images and Archive Photography, Bill Niven, Petty Enterprises.

A Note About Statistics: The statistics quoted in *NASCAR: A Fast History* have been compiled by the author. Many of the numbers do not match official statistics recognized by NASCAR, but they do represent the best efforts of one of racing's most respected historians.

Contents

Before
NASCAR ▶▶

Beach Trials

The original speed trials on the hardpacked sands along the shore of the Atlantic Ocean took place in Ormond Beach, just north of Daytona Beach, as early as 1902. They continued until 1935 before moving to Bonneville, Utah. Triumph and tragedy marked the trials. Frank Lockhart's 183-cid V-16-powered Stutz Blackhawk (far left) pierced the Measured Mile at 198.292 mph in 1928. When a tire blew on the return run, the car tumbled and Lockhart was killed instantly. Also in '28, Ray Keech piloted Jim White's 36-cylinder Triplex (left), tying two runs together at 207.552 mph for a new world's Land Speed Record. Keech vowed to never drive the ill-handling Triplex again. The following year, Lee Bible lost his life behind the wheel of the Triplex. The final car to run on the beach was Sir Malcolm Campbell's Bluebird V (below), a 30-foot-long, five-ton beast with a 2227-cid, 2700-horse-power engine. Campbell ran a 276.82 mph two-way average on March 7, 1935, with a one-way run of over 330 mph. On the return run, part of the cowling ripped away. Campbell spun sideways, but was unhurt.

The First Beach Race

A variety of stock automobiles competed in the inaugural auto race at Daytona Beach on March 8, 1936. Coupes, hardtops, sports cars, and convertibles were all eligible. Many of the speedier but heavier cars got bogged down in the sandy corners, while the nifty Fords sailed over the ruts with relative ease and claimed the top six spots. Here, wealthy sportsman Jack Rutherford guides his #29 Auburn bobtail speedster through the rutted north turn. Rutherford failed to finish the car-killing contest. Only 10 cars in the starting field of 27 were running when officials halted the race 10 miles short of its scheduled 250-mile distance. Milt Marion (inset) was flagged the winner in his '36 Ford and collected the $1700 top prize. A young Bill France finished fifth.

Lloyd Seay

NASCAR founder Bill France, Sr., regarded Lloyd Seay as the "greatest stock car driver who ever lived." That praise is made more remarkable by the fact that Lloyd Seay never competed in a NASCAR race. He was murdered nearly eight years before NASCAR was incorporated. "I raced against Lloyd before the war," France said in 1984. "He was the best pure driver I ever saw, and I have seen 'em all."

Seay was born in the north Georgia hills on Dec. 14, 1919. An adventurous sort, Seay grew up on the rough side of the tracks and fell in with lawless characters. In his early teens, Seay became involved in whiskey tripping, transporting "hooch"—usually with the police and revenue agents in hot pursuit. His exploits behind the wheel of a car on the twisting switchback roads of Georgia became legend. "He was wide open all the way," said Raymond Parks, a tycoon among race-team owners before and immediately after the war.

Seay's ability to hang a car on the edge made him an instant threat to win races, particularly with the support of Parks and Red Vogt, the game's top mechanic. At the age of 18, Seay entered his first stock car race at Atlanta's Lakewood Speedway—and prevailed.

Seay's rise to stardom was meteoric. In 1941, Seay won three races of national importance, the Aug. 24 race on Daytona's Beach-Road course, the Aug. 31 race at High Point, N.C., and the annual championship event at Lakewood Speedway in Atlanta on Sept. 1.

Only hours after his third win in 15 days, Lloyd Seay was shot to death by his cousin, Woodrow Anderson. According to police reports, the two argued over sugar Seay had purchased on Anderson's credit.

Raymond Parks arranged for an unusual tombstone to rest over Seay's burial place. Seay's famous #7 Ford coupe was engraved in relief and the driver's window was carved out. Inserted in its place was a photo of Seay, mounted in a crystal cube.

Largely unknown today, Lloyd Seay generated excitement and showed fans what stock car racing was all about simply by how he drove a race car.

The National Championship Stock Car Circuit

In early 1947, Bill France announced the formation of the National Championship Stock Car Circuit, a new stock car touring series. France saw the potential of a unified series. It was time for the sport to grow beyond its Southern roots.

France had first approached the American Automobile Association to include stock car racing in its repertoire of auto-racing sanctions. In exchange for AAA group insurance and sanction, France wanted to conduct a stock car racing series under the AAA banner. Effectively, the AAA told France to get lost.

Undaunted, France carried on by himself. Predictably, about a half dozen other organizations formed to grab a piece of the action. By organizing a series of races with points standings and a standard set of rules, France put himself one step ahead of the competition. The NCSCC's top points winners would share in postseason money. A thousand bucks and a trophy were promised to the champion.

France's new circuit began in January 1947 at Daytona Beach and concluded at Jacksonville in December, having sanctioned nearly 40 events. Attendance at most races exceeded capacity. Posted awards were paid, points accumulated, and a champion was named. Fonty Flock logged seven wins in 24 starts en route to a narrow victory over Ed Samples and Red Byron in the NCSCC championship chase.

Just as he had promised, Bill France delivered the postseason payoff. Flock

received a huge four-foot trophy and $1000. A total of $3000 was doled out to the top drivers. The season was deemed a success, but greater accomplishment was on the horizon as the NCSCC would evolve into a new circuit called NASCAR.

15

The Streamline Hotel and the Birth of NASCAR

During the final weeks of the 1947 National Championship Stock Car Circuit season, Bill France spread the word to track operators, drivers, owners, and any interested party that a big powwow would take place in December in Daytona Beach. Big Bill, a man of strong will, wanted to take the sport to a national level, but he knew he needed the support of the contestants. He welcomed all to the Streamline Hotel for a series of meetings that began on Dec. 14, 1947.

Thirty-five men gathered at 1:00 P.M. that Sunday afternoon on the top floor of the Streamline Hotel, and France called to order the "First Annual Convention of the National Championship Stock Car Circuit." The meeting was the first of four days of seminars that would outline the direction of stock car racing. During the meeting, France said: "Gentlemen, right here within our group rests the outcome of stock car racing in the country today. We have the opportunity to set it up on a big scale. We are all interested in one thing: improving present conditions."

Bill Tuthill, a racing promoter from New York, became France's right-hand lieutenant, as well as the chairman of the meetings. By the end of the seminars, France had appointed technical and competition committees with all factions—drivers, mechanics, and owners—represented. Louis Vogt, ace-mechanic of the era, coined the name for the organization: National Association for Stock Car Auto Racing—NASCAR. Houston Lawing was appointed publicity director. Everyone seemed to think France's new circuit was a good idea.

One of the most important elements to come out of the meetings was an insurance policy and a benevolent fund for injured drivers. With assistance from Daytona Beach attorney Louis Ossinski, NASCAR was formed into a private corporation with France as President. E. G. "Cannonball" Baker, a well-respected racer from the Roaring '20s, was appointed National Commissioner.

NASCAR also expanded to include regional series in the Northeast and Midwest. The series began with a 62½-mile race at Pompano Beach on Jan. 4, 1948, and continues to this day as the most successful form of racing in North America.

the 1940s ▶▶

Early Modifieds, Dusty Battles

Thick, blinding dust billows off the churning tires of the NASCAR Modifieds during a 35-mile race at Hillsboro's Occoneechee Speedway on June 19, 1948. A total of 36 cars entered the race, which was the 12th of the 1949 Modified season, and Fonty Flock scored his seventh win. Customary procedure for the Modified card included time trials, a pair of heat races, a consolation event, a semifeature, and, finally, the main event. Modifieds were the only cars to run in the 1948 NASCAR season. Late-model stock cars wouldn't debut until the middle of the 1949 campaign.

Occoneechee Opens

The one-mile Occoneechee Speedway presented its inaugural race on June 27, 1948. The NASCAR Modifieds competed in a 100-mile jaunt, one of the biggest events on the '48 calendar. Here, Jack Etheridge cocks his #6 Ford into the corner, just ahead of #7/11 Sara Christian. Others pictured are #7 Frank Mundy, #14 Bob Flock, and #44 Marshall Teague. Fonty Flock beat Teague to take the victory.

1948

Red Byron

Red Byron, a decorated war hero, prevailed in an intense battle for the 1948 NASCAR championship after a season-long struggle with '47 NCSCC title winner Fonty Flock. Byron grabbed the points lead in the 49th of 52 national championship races and edged Flock by 32.75 points.

Byron won 11 races, including four in a row in April and May. Flock finished first in 15 races, including six wins in the final two months.

Byron and Flock swapped the points lead five times during the season. Byron snared the lead for keeps after winning the Oct. 17 race at North Wilkesboro.

Young Tim Flock wound up third in the points standings, followed by seven-time winner Curtis Turner and two-race winner Buddy Shuman.

Red Byron
#22 Ford
Owner: Raymond Parks

Starts	34
Wins	11
Top 5	25
Top 10	32
Points	2996.50
Winnings	$13,150

The First Strictly Stock Race

Prior to World War II, nearly every stock car race featured late-model sedans. After the war, a shortage of new, postwar cars prevented late-model racing—until May 1949, when Bill France decided he would conduct a "Strictly Stock" race.

Charlotte Speedway was chosen to host the 150-mile race for stock late-model cars. The field for the June 19, 1949, Strictly Stock race would be open to the fastest 33 cars in qualifications, *à la* the Indianapolis 500.

Many of the cars were driven to the track, and less than 30 had entered. Plenty of new American cars were parked in the infield, though. Tim Flock spotted a '49 Oldsmobile 88 and talked the owner, Buddy Elliott, into letting him drive the Olds in the race. Glenn Dunnaway found a 1947 Ford owned by Hubert Westmoreland, and he, too, got a ride just before qualifying. Dunnaway was told the car may be a moonshine runner, which probably meant it was pretty fast.

In the final laps, Dunnaway drove his bootlegger Ford past Jim Roper's sputtering #34 Lincoln and cruised to victory. He earned $2000 from the overall purse of $6000. Roper held on for second.

After the race, the NASCAR technical committee, headed by Al Crisler, thoroughly inspected the top cars. Crisler found that the winning 1947 Ford was equipped with stiffened springs. Custom work on an automobile's springs was essential to deliver moonshine quickly, and the better traction it afforded in the corners figured prominently in Dunnaway's win. But stiffened springs weren't allowed by the Strictly Stock guidelines. Crisler disqualified the car with Bill France's blessing, and Jim Roper became the first winner on the circuit that would become the NASCAR NEXTEL Cup Series. Westmoreland later challenged the ruling in court, but the case was dismissed.

Women Drivers

NASCAR drivers have always been viewed as "good ol' boys," but over the years a few women have driven at NASCAR's highest level. Sara Christian was the most famous female racer in the early days. The Atlanta housewife ran in the first NASCAR Strictly Stock race and competed in six of the eight Strictly Stock events in the inaugural 1949 season. Her fifth-place finish at Pittsburgh's Heidelberg Speedway remains the best finish for a female driver in NASCAR's top division. Ethel Flock Mobley drove in two Strictly Stock events in '49, winning a total of $50. Louise Smith competed in 11 races between '49 and '52, never placing in the top ten. Over the years, a dozen more female racers have tackled the NASCAR tour. In the '50s, Ann Bunselmeyer, Ann Chester, Marion Pagan, Ann Slaasted, and Fifi Scott all made brief appearances. In the '60s, only Goldie Parsons made a single appearance. Janet Guthrie made 33 starts between '76 and '80, including the July 4, 1977, Firecracker 400 at Daytona that also featured female drivers Lella Lombardi and Christine Beckers. Since then, Robin McCall, Patty Moise, and Shawna Robinson have qualified. Robinson made the most appearances, competing in eight events in 2001 and '02, including the '02 Daytona 500.

Clockwise from top left: Ethel Flock Mobley with brother Fonty Flock; Janet Guthrie's #68 Kelly Girl Chevrolet at the 1977 Darlington Southern 500; Janet Guthrie, Lella Lombardi, Lee Petty, Christine Beckers, and Louise Smith [left to right] at the 1977 Firecracker 500; Sara Christian. Opposite: Louise Smith.

1949
Red Byron

Red Byron won his second straight NASCAR title and became the first champion of the new Strictly Stock late-model tour on the strength of a pair of wins during the abbreviated eight-race campaign. Byron finished 117.5 points in front of runner-up Lee Petty, who won once.

Byron took the lead in the points standings after his victory at Daytona Beach, the second Strictly Stock race of the inaugural season. His second victory at Martinsville in September locked up the title.

Byron drove Oldsmobiles for Raymond Parks during the campaign. Chief mechanic Red Vogt kept the cars in top running order all season. Byron only finished out of the top 10 in two of his six starts.

Two-time winner Bob Flock came in third, with Bill Blair and Fonty Flock rounding out the top five.

Red Byron
#22 Oldsmobile
Owner: Raymond Parks

Starts	6
Wins	2
Top 5	4
Top 10	4
Points	842.50
Winnings	$5800

the 1950s ▶▶▶

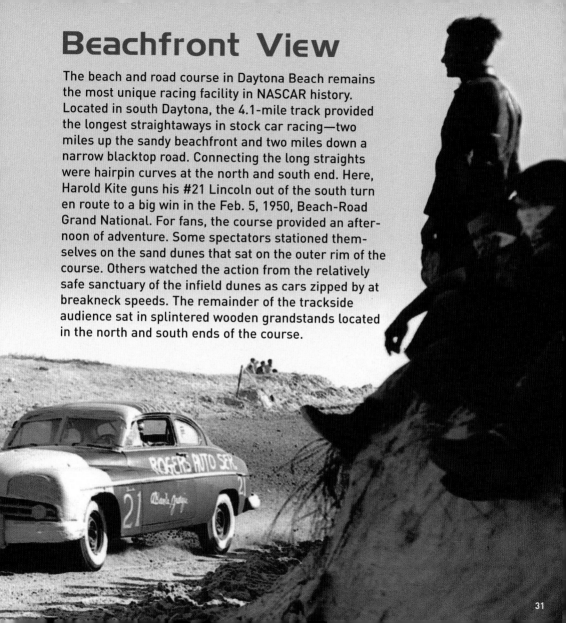

Beachfront View

The beach and road course in Daytona Beach remains the most unique racing facility in NASCAR history. Located in south Daytona, the 4.1-mile track provided the longest straightaways in stock car racing—two miles up the sandy beachfront and two miles down a narrow blacktop road. Connecting the long straights were hairpin curves at the north and south end. Here, Harold Kite guns his #21 Lincoln out of the south turn en route to a big win in the Feb. 5, 1950, Beach-Road Grand National. For fans, the course provided an afternoon of adventure. Some spectators stationed themselves on the sand dunes that sat on the outer rim of the course. Others watched the action from the relatively safe sanctuary of the infield dunes as cars zipped by at breakneck speeds. The remainder of the trackside audience sat in splintered wooden grandstands located in the north and south ends of the course.

Fans' Race

The promoters at North Carolina's North Wilkesboro Speedway conducted the "Wilkes County Championship Fan's Car Race" to accompany the June 11, 1950, NASCAR Modified race. The cars didn't have race graphics and all had been driven to the event (note the license plates). Third-place starter Gwyn Staley, brother of North Wilkesboro Speedway promoter Enoch Staley, won the 10-lap race in a pickup truck.

Inaugural Southern Five Hundred

Seventy-five cars lined up three-abreast on Labor Day, Sept. 4, 1950, for the inaugural Southern Five-Hundred at Harold Brasington's brand-new Darlington Raceway. Curtis Turner, Jimmy Thompson, and Gober Sosebee qualified for the front row. Johnny Mantz drove the #98JR. 1950 Plymouth to victory. The black Plymouth, which was owned by Bill France, Alvin Hawkins, and Hubert Westmoreland, had been used as a utility vehicle during the two weeks leading up to the Southern Five-Hundred. Mantz used durable truck tires in the race and cruised to victory by nine full laps when his speedier rivals had to make several pit stops to replace blown tires.

1950

NASCAR GRAND NATIONAL CHAMPION

Bill Rexford

Despite mechanical problems in the season finale at Hillsboro, N.C., 23-year-old Bill Rexford held off Fireball Roberts by an eyelash to capture the 1950 NASCAR Grand National championship.

The 1950 title chase was quite memorable. In the 19-race campaign, the points lead changed hands nine times among seven different drivers. Rexford took the points lead in the next-to-last race at Winchester, Ind., and finished 110.5 points ahead of Roberts.

Roberts, the 21-year-old youngster from Daytona Beach, could have won the title with a fifth-place finish in the season finale. With Rexford on the sidelines, Fireball elected to charge to the front rather than employ a conservative approach. Roberts led twice for nine laps, but blew the engine in his Oldsmobile and wound up 21st.

In addition to Rexford and Roberts, others to lead the standings during the season included Curtis Turner, Lloyd Moore, Tim Flock, Red Byron, and Harold Kite.

Bill Rexford
#8, 20, 59, 60, 62, 80
Ford, Mercury, Oldsmobile
Owner: Julian Buesink

Starts	17
Wins	1
Top 5	5
Top 10	11
Points	1959
Winnings	$6175

War of Attrition

Herb Thomas takes the checkered flag in winning the July 15, 1951, event at Heidelberg Speedway near Pittsburgh. Thomas hooked up with Oldsmobile team owner Hubert Westmoreland for this one event. The 100-mile race was one of the most brutal in NASCAR history. The starting field consisted of 42 cars, but only five finished. Many were wiped out in a series of wrecks. Dust conditions were particularly bad that afternoon, which adversely affected the drivers' vision.

NASCAR Invades Motor City

The Aug. 12, 1951, Motor City 250 at Detroit's Michigan State Fairgrounds was one of the most important races in NASCAR history. It was the first time NASCAR's unique brand of stock car racing played out on the auto industry's doorstep, and the race couldn't have been more thrilling. Many cars were retired in what turned out to be a slugfest, including Bill Holland's #175 Cadillac (right). Newcomer Tommy Thompson, driving the #40 Chrysler, locked horns with Curtis Turner in the final laps. Dueling for the lead, the big Chrysler and Turner's Olds collided in the third turn. As they zoomed down the front chute, Turner's busted radiator spit out a geyser of steam, leaving Thompson with a clear path to victory (below right). A wall-to-wall crowd of 16,352 witnessed the action-packed contest, and to NASCAR's delight, the automobile executives took a keen interest, too. Factory involvement followed within the next few years.

41

1951
Herb Thomas

With his victory in Darlington's Labor Day Southern 500, Herb Thomas leapt atop the NASCAR Grand National points standings and led the rest of the season. Thomas, winner of seven races during the 41-race season, finished only 146.2 points ahead of runner-up Fonty Flock, who won eight races.

Thomas was within striking distance of the points lead throughout the first half of the season, but didn't take the lead until his big win at Darlington, when he earned 1250 points. The distribution of points in 1951 was parallel to the posted awards, and the Southern 500 was the richest race on the schedule. Fonty Flock finished eighth at Darlington, earning 375 points.

The points lead changed hands nine times among four drivers during the season. Tim Flock finished third after leading the standings for 13 races. Lee Petty and Frank Mundy rounded out the top five.

Herb Thomas
#2, 6, 41, 92 Hudson, Plymouth
Owners: Herb Thomas, Hubert Westmoreland, Marshall Teague, Leonard Tippett

Starts	35
Wins	7
Top 5	16
Top 10	18
Points	4208.45
Winnings	$21,050

NASCAR's Speedway Division

The NASCAR Speedway Division ran its second race at Martinsville Speedway on May 25, 1952. Only 17 cars were ready for the 100-miler, but the new open-wheel cars generated a pretty good crowd. Bill Miller is in the pole slot in his "Olds 88 Special." Flanking him on the outside is Buddy Shuman in the "GMC Special." Tex Keene, in an open wheeler powered by a stock Mercury engine, came from his 16th starting spot to win the race. A total of seven Speedway Division events were staged in 1952, and Buck Baker was crowned champion. The division returned in '53 with only a few heat races, then fizzled out.

Brothers Behind the Wheel

The 1952 NASCAR Grand National season was a family affair. Two sets of brothers made much of the news this year. Herb Thomas (below left) won eight races and finished a close second in the championship points race. Herb's 20-year-old brother, Donald (below right), became the youngest winner in NASCAR Grand National history (a record that still stands) with his Nov. 16 victory at Atlanta's Lakewood Speedway. Donald started the race, then turned his car over to Herb, who drove it to victory. According to the rules, Donald got credit for the win, and Herb accumulated championship points.

   Bob Flock (opposite left with brother Fonty) missed the first half of the 1952 schedule with a broken neck suffered in the '51 season finale. Flock made a memorable comeback by winning his first race back, the Aug. 17, 1952, event at Weaverville, N.C. Fonty Flock (opposite bottom), known for his race-day attire of shorts and a polo shirt, won the Southern 500 and finished fourth in the title chase. Brother Tim (opposite right) drove the Ted Chester-owned Hudson Hornet to the 1952 NASCAR Grand National championship.

1952
Tim Flock

The battle for the 1952 championship came down to the final event of the season at West Palm Beach. Tim Flock, who took the points lead from Herb Thomas at Langhorne in September, clinched the title by simply starting the 100-miler. Flock smacked the wall and flipped down the front chute in the West Palm Beach finale, but he had accumulated enough points to seal the championship.

"I think I'm the only guy who ever won a championship on his head," cracked Flock afterward.

Thomas, who had taken the points lead at Darlington, only held it for two races before Flock was back in front. The final margin was 106 points.

Flock and Thomas both won eight races during the 34-race campaign. Lee Petty, Fonty Flock, and Dick Rathmann, all multiple race winners, filled out the top five in the final NASCAR Grand National standings.

Tim Flock
#91 Hudson
Owner: Ted Chester

Starts	33
Wins	8
Top 5	22
Top 10	25
Points	6858.50
Winnings	$22,890

Illegal Assist

Fonty Flock seemingly drove his #14 Oldsmobile to victory in the
Feb. 15, Daytona Beach Grand National race, but lost due to a rules
violation. Flock ran out of gas on the final lap and was pushed
across the finish line by teammate Slick Smith. NASCAR disallowed
the assist and awarded Flock second place. Bill Blair capitalized on
Flock's bad luck, driving his #2 Olds to victory. Although he never
passed Flock, Blair's victory is recorded as the first NASCAR Grand
National race to be determined by a last-lap pass.

Jocko Flocko, Monkey Copilot

Early in the 1953 NASCAR Grand National season, Hudson team owner Ted Chester hatched a crazy idea. He thought teaming a rhesus monkey with lead driver Tim Flock would be a great gimmick.

"Ted came to me and told me about this monkey he wanted to put in the race car with me," reflected Tim Flock years later. "I thought Ted had been hittin' the jug too much. But the more I got to thinking about it, the more I liked it. Ted said the monkey already had the name 'Jocko,' and he gave him a last name of 'Flocko.' I decided Jocko Flocko could ride with me anytime."

Chester rigged a small seat for Jocko, had a seamstress sew a well-fitted uniform, and even provided a small helmet for him.

Jocko Flocko rode with Tim Flock in eight races, including a win in the May 16, 1953, race at Hickory.

Two weeks later, Jocko competed in his final race. "Before we had special

NASCAR Grand National Career Record 1953
Starts: 8
Wins: 1
Top 5s: 1
Top 10s: 6
Poles: 0
Career Winnings: $3945

durable racing tires, there was a cable attached to a trap door over the right front wheelwell," said Flock. During the race, the driver would pull on the cable, which would open the trap door so we could check the tire wear.

"In the 300-mile race at Raleigh, we had a little problem with Jocko. Late in the race, while I was running second, he broke loose from his seat and he jumped down on the floorboard. He yanked that cable and opened the trap door—right as I ran over a rock on the track. The rock zinged Jocko right between the eyes. He went crazy. He jumped on my neck and started scratching me to the point I almost wrecked a couple of times. Finally, I had to make a pit stop so we could put Jocko out of the car. I'm the only driver in NASCAR history to lose a race because we had to pit to get rid of a monkey," Flock said with a chuckle.

Publicity Machine

From the very beginning, Bill France and NASCAR recognized the importance of exposure. In 1953, NASCAR began issuing staged publicity photographs of mock racing action to local newspapers. Accompanying a prerace press release, photos like this showed up on the desks of local sports editors a couple weeks in advance of an upcoming race. Cars were parked sideways on a track, wheels cocked to the right to depict the action readers might see if they attended a NASCAR Grand National event. Here, the cars of Fonty Flock (#14), Herb Thomas (#92), Tim Flock (#91), and Curtis Turner (#41) sit idle on an undisclosed track.

1953

Herb Thomas

Herb Thomas took the lead in the 1953 points standings in early March and never looked back as he sailed to his second NASCAR Grand National championship. The Olivia, N.C., driver won 12 events in the 37-race season and finished a comfortable 646 points ahead of runner-up Lee Petty, who won five races.

Thomas and crew chief Smokey Yunick were true to the test of an exhaustive schedule. In July and the first week in August, the tour made stops in New York, South Carolina, New Jersey, Georgia, South Dakota, Nebraska, Iowa, and North Carolina—in that order! Thomas won four races during that stretch.

Thomas led virtually every category during his championship run. He won the most races, led the most laps, scored the most top-five and top-10 finishes, completed the most miles, and set a record with $28,909.58 in prize money and postseason awards.

Herb Thomas
#92 Hudson
Owner: Herb Thomas

Starts	37
Wins	12
Top 5	27
Top 10	31
Points	8460
Winnings	$28,909

Tim Flock DQ'd, Quits

Tim Flock motored to a convincing victory in the Feb 21, 1954, Daytona Beach Grand National event. Upon a postrace inspection, however, NASCAR technical director Jim Ross discovered that the venturis in Flock's carburetor had been relieved ⅛ inch. Ross disqualified Flock and declared runner-up Lee Petty the official winner. Flock responded by quitting the NASCAR circuit in a huff and going home to Atlanta to operate a gas station. Team Owner Ernest Woods put Tim's brother Bob in his Helzapopin' Oldsmobile (inset, right) for the March 28 race at Savannah, Ga. Woods simply whitewashed Tim's name from the roof, leaving "Flock." Buck Baker and Jim Paschal drove the Woods car for most of the rest of the season, even when Tim Flock returned to the circuit for the Sept. 12 race at Macon, Ga. Flock, the 1952 champion, competed in only five races in 1954.

Those Fabulous Hudson Hornets

Hudson introduced its "Step-down"-design cars in 1948. The driver and passengers stepped down into the car, rather than up onto the floorboard. This unibody design had a low center of gravity that afforded superior handling. Still, Hudsons were largely overlooked by NASCAR drivers until the release of the 1951 Hudson Hornet, which featured a powerful 308-cid "H-145" straight six that made 145 horsepower. NASCAR competitors soon took notice and the results were amazing.

Hudsons began winning NASCAR Grand National races with regularity, and drivers sang the Hornet's praises. In a 1952 booklet entitled *Why the Fabulous Hudson Hornet is a Winner*, NASCAR veteran Marshall Teague noted that the "Monobilt body-and-frame gives Hudson structural rigidity or just plain ruggedness that no other car has." In that same booklet, Herb Thomas said he gained a lot of distance in turns. Thomas drove a Hudson to the 1951 NASCAR Grand National championship, winning seven races. Overall, Hornets won a dozen races that year.

Of the 34 NASCAR Grand National races run in 1952, Hudson won 27. Tim Flock took the title behind the wheel of a Hudson. Over the next two years, Hudson won 39 of 74 races. Herb Thomas drove a Hudson to the '53 title, but Lee Petty broke Hudson's three-year string by claiming the '54 crown driving mostly Dodges.

By 1955, rival automakers had designed more-powerful, lightweight vehicles, and the Fords, Chryslers, and Chevys rolling off assembly lines were ideal for racing. Hudson had made only peripheral changes to the Hornet in '55, and virtually every Hudson driver switched to Hudson's competitors.

Hudson never won a NASCAR Grand National race after February 1955. But for four years, the Hudson Hornet ruled the stock car racing world.

1951

1952

HUDSON HORNETS SET ALL-TIME STOCK CAR RECORD!

31 VICTORIES IN 35 STARTS!
Never in history has one car given such a positive demonstration of superiority

Why the Fabulous HUDSON HORNET is a Winner

By Marshall Teague and Herb Thomas

1953

1954

NASCAR's First Road Course

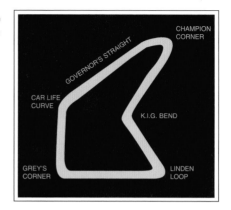

Upon its inception, NASCAR's Grand National circuit drivers made only left-hand turns, usually on flat dirt tracks. Paved tracks were gradually added to the mix, but they were still ovals. It wasn't until June 13, 1954, that the competitors tackled their first road course. That's when promoters Ed Otto and Red Crise organized an "International 100 Mile Race."

Otto and Crise developed a two-mile, five-turn course on the concrete runways and taxiways on the Linden, N.J., airport. To add interest, foreign cars were made eligible for NASCAR's maiden voyage into road-racing waters.

Foreign cars weren't unheard of in NASCAR competition. On rare occasions, NASCAR had permitted foreign sports cars to compete on the Grand National circuit. The most notable achievement was Lloyd Moore's Jaguar winning the pole for the June 21, 1953, race at Langhorne, Penn.; a race won by Dick Rathmann in a Hudson. That event featured ten foreign makes. Domestic cars took the first five positions, and a Volkswagen managed to finish 19th in the field of 38.

For the Linden event, Otto-Crise Promotions decided to promote a race within a race, awarding a bonus for the best-finishing foreign sports car equipped with an engine smaller than 2000 cubic centimeters (about 122 cid).

The two-mile course consisted of four left-hand turns and a single right-hand bend. Total posted awards of $5020 attracted a full field of cars. Twenty-one foreign cars and 22 domestic stock cars qualified for starting spots. A total of 13 different makes started the race. Nimble Jaguars, MGs, Morgans, Austin-Healeys, and a Porsche lined up next to the full-size domestic Hudsons, Oldsmobiles, Dodges, Plymouths, and Fords. Even a couple of tiny Henry Js were entered.

New Yorker Al Keller, a part-time NASCAR driver since 1948, qualified seventh in a Jaguar coupe owned by bandleader Paul Whiteman. Keller breezed into the lead just before the halfway point and scampered away from the field in his lightweight Jaguar to claim an easy victory. Joe Eubanks finished second in a Hudson, and Buck Baker placed third. Jaguars took the next three spots.

A crowd of nearly 10,000 turned out for the event, making it a success. Still, it would be another two-and-a-half years before the NASCAR Grand Nationals would again compete on a road course. Road-course racing never did become NASCAR Grand National racing's stock and trade, and a foreign car never won again.

1954
Lee Petty

Parlaying consistency, Lee Petty took the points lead in mid May and cruised to a 283-point victory in the NASCAR Grand National championship race.

Two-time champion Herb Thomas gave chase but was unable to catch the smooth-driving Petty, despite 12 wins to Petty's eight. Buck Baker, who led the standings for six weeks in early spring, wound up third in the standings on the strength of four wins.

Petty started the season strong with a win in the Feb. 21 Daytona Beach NASCAR Grand National race. He only finished out of the top five in 10 races. The 1954 championship was sweet revenge for Petty, who lost the '50 title when NASCAR docked him 849 points for competing in a non-NASCAR-sanctioned event.

Lee Petty
#42 Dodge, Chrysler, Oldsmobile
Owners: Petty Engineering, Gary Drake

Starts	34
Wins	7
Top 5	24
Top 10	32
Points	8649
Winnings	$21,101

Chevrolet's First Win

Fonty Flock cuts a quick lap ahead of an unnumbered Buick on a dirt track in 1955. Flock recorded the first NASCAR Grand National win for Chevrolet on March 26 at Columbia, S.C. Frank Christian owned the car and secured sponsorship from Carl Kiekhaefer's Mercury Outboards. Later in the '55 season, Fonty joined the Kiekhaefer Chrysler team when Christian folded his operation. Herb Thomas earned Chevy its second win on Sept. 5, when he piloted the Smokey Yunick-owned #92 Motoramic Chevy to victory in Darlington's Southern 500. Thomas was swamped in victory lane.

1955
Tim Flock

Tim Flock thoroughly dominated the 1955 NASCAR Grand National season, winning 18 races in 38 starts along the way to his second championship in four years. Flock finished 1508 points in front of runner-up Buck Baker, but he didn't take the points lead until the season's 33rd race in mid August.

Consistent Lee Petty led the points standings most of the season but was no match for Flock, who drove the powerful Kiekhaefer Chryslers. Petty's consistency kept him on top of the points standings, but he tapered off in the second half of the season. Petty won six races and wound up third in the final standings.

Herb Thomas rallied back from injuries suffered at Charlotte that cost him three months of the season, and finished fifth in the standings.

Flock's record of 18 wins wouldn't be surpassed until 1967 when Richard Petty won 27 races.

Tim Flock
#300, 301, 16 Chrysler;
#2 Chevrolet
Owners: Carl Kiekhaefer,
Hubert Westmoreland

Starts	39
Wins	18
Top 5	32
Top 10	33
Points	9596
Winnings	$37,779

The NASCAR Convertible Division

Looking to add a new division to NASCAR, Bill France thought a convertible circuit started in 1955 by the Indianapolis-based Society of Autosports, Fellowship and Education (SAFE) could be the answer. So NASCAR and SAFE joined forces, and the SAFE All Star Circuit of Champions became the NASCAR Convertible Division at the start of the 1956 season. The new circuit staged 47 races in 17 states and Canada in '56. Bob Welborn, who drove the #49 Chevrolet, won the championship while winning three races. Curtis Turner won 22 races, but came in a distant second in the points chase due in part to having missed five races. The convertible tour lasted only four full seasons. It lost momentum when hardtops outclassed the convertibles in the inaugural Daytona 500 in 1959, and folded after that season.

Truelove's Tumble

Russ Truelove's tumble midway through the Feb. 26, 1956, Daytona Beach NASCAR Grand National was one of the most spectacular in beach-racing history. Truelove's Mercury was one of the quickest cars, qualifying fifth. The beach conditions were awful, though. Truelove hit a soft patch in the sand and flipped almost a dozen times near the north end of the beach. Afterward, Truelove stepped out of the smoldering machine through the passenger door. At the right, photographers and Truelove (middle) examine the spectacular sequence.

Team Kiekhaefer

Carl Kiekhaefer, founder of the Mercury Outboard division, entered NASCAR Grand National racing in 1955 and immediately became a powerful force.

Tim Flock drove a Kiekhaefer Chrysler to 18 wins and the 1955 NASCAR Grand National title. However, Flock couldn't take Kiekhaefer's drill-sergeant attitude and quit the Kiekhaefer team early in '56. Still, the Kiekhaefer cars won 30 races in '56, 14 of them by lead driver Buck Baker, who also won the championship.

Fielding as many as six cars at a time, Kiekhaefer's domination caused controversy. His teams were booed, and, in his opinion, hassled by the media and competitors.

Kiekhaefer's fate was sealed late in 1956. With Baker trailing rival Herb Thomas, who had quit the Kiekhaefer team at midseason, Kiekhaefer leased a track in Shelby, N.C., and arranged for NASCAR's sanction. In the race, Kiekhaefer driver Speedy Thompson hooked Thomas' bumper and caused him to crash. Thomas was critically injured and Baker rode home uncontested as the '56 champion.

Fearing that negative reaction would damage his Mercury Outboard empire, Kiekhaefer never appeared at another NASCAR race. His legacy and records remain to this day, and it is unlikely any team can match the marks Carl Kiekhaefer set in 1955 and '56.

**KIEKHAEFER
NASCAR
Grand National
Record
1955-1956**
Starts: 190 (90 races)
Wins: 51
Top 5s: 116
Top 10s: 138
Poles: 51
Career Winnings:
$135,681

1956
Buck Baker

A horrendous crash took Herb Thomas out of the championship hunt late in the season, allowing Buck Baker to cruise to the 1956 NASCAR Grand National title. Thomas, leading the points race entering the October race at Shelby, N.C., suffered critical injuries in a multicar crash on the ½-mile dirt track.

Speedy Thompson, Baker's teammate on the Carl Kiekhaefer team, triggered the crash and considerable controversy. Thomas, who quit the Kiekhaefer team at midseason, had taken the points lead a month earlier.

Thompson drew the wrath of observers and sportswriters for causing the crash that injured Thomas. Team owner Kiekhaefer was also extensively criticized by the media. Baker was exonerated of any alleged "team play" in the race.

Baker won 14 races and his first NASCAR title, finishing 484 points ahead of runner-up Thompson.

Buck Baker
#87, 31 Ford;
#00, 31, 87, 300, 300B,
300C, 301, 500B, 501, 502
Chrysler, Dodge
Owners: Carl Kiekhaefer,
Satcher Motors

Starts	48
Wins	14
Top 5	31
Top 10	39
Points	9272
Winnings	$34,076

Pontiac's First Win

Number 6 Cotton Owens leads #87 Buck Baker and #61 Dick Foley in the early stages of the Feb. 17, 1957, Daytona Beach NASCAR Grand National race. Owens drove a Pontiac owned and prepared by Ray Nichels, who was campaigning in his first big NASCAR event. Owens won the race, giving Pontiac its first win in NASCAR Grand National competition.

Smokey Yunick

Henry Yunick, better known as "Smokey," had perhaps the most innovative mind in NASCAR history. He was known for his technological "creations," bordering on genius, along with slick methods of skirting around NASCAR rules.

Long before the age of the wind tunnel, Smokey was able to gather visual evidence of the effects of wind currents on an automobile at high speed. He would often carve a small-scale model of a stock car in wood, and set the replica in a running stream. Yunick noted how the water rippled around the contours of the model and estimated how that would translate onto the high-banked speedways.

Smokey often tested NASCAR rules by adding aerodynamic pieces of sheet-metal to offset turbulence. As an example, he added fender flares to a '67 Chevelle, a car that Curtis Turner piloted to the pole position for the Daytona 500.

Yunick was quite liberal with his interpretation of the rules. While NASCAR set a 22-gallon limit for all fuel tanks, there was no mention of the filler neck. Yunick always complied with the regulation 22-gallon fuel limit, but his filler necks often snaked throughout the rear of his cars, holding several extra gallons. It wasn't cheating, Yunick reasoned, because there was no rule with regard against it.

Yunick won only a handful of races as a team owner, but that statistic is misleading. While he built and prepared the Pontiac that Fireball Roberts used to sweep Daytona's Speedweeks events in 1962, dealership owner Jim Stephens is credited as the winning team owner. Another Pontiac dealership owner, John Hine, is credited for winning the inaugural NASCAR race at Atlanta's superspeedway in 1960, though the car was handcrafted and entered by Yunick. Smokey won 48 NASCAR Grand National races as a crew chief, but only eight as an owner.

Serving as pit boss in 1953, Smokey guided Herb Thomas to the NASCAR Grand National championship. Yunick won races with legends such as Fireball Roberts and Paul Goldsmith, but also garnered wins with inexperienced drivers Johnny Rutherford (in his very first NASCAR start in 1963) and Donald Thomas (the youngest winner in NASCAR history in 1952).

Smokey often battled with Bill France over the rules and left NASCAR after the 1969 season. He has often been referred to as NASCAR's most colorful mechanic, but he was also the most gifted individual to ever turn a wrench on a stock car.

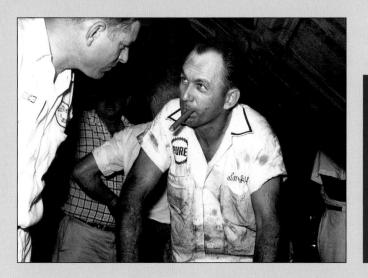

**SMOKEY YUNICK
NASCAR
Grand National
Career Record
1956-1969**
Starts: 61
Wins: 8
Top 5s: 22
Top 10s: 30
Poles: 9
Career Winnings:
$79,413

1957

Buck Baker

Buck Baker assumed command of the 1957 points race in mid May and easily won his second straight NASCAR Grand National championship. Baker finished 760 points ahead of Marvin Panch, who led the points standings for the first 16 races.

Baker was consistently excellent throughout the season. He began the year with 26 consecutive top-10 finishes and finished the campaign with 38 top-10 efforts in 40 starts. The veteran from Charlotte, N.C., won 10 races along the way in his Chevrolet.

Panch won six races in 42 starts during his first full NASCAR Grand National season, including the opening two events. He led the points standings until the May 19 race at Martinsville, when Baker took the points lead with a victory.

Two-time winner Speedy Thompson finished third in the points race, followed by Lee Petty and Jack Smith, who both won four events.

Buck Baker
#87 Chevrolet
Owners: Buck Baker,
Hugh Babb

Starts	39
Wins	18
Top 5	32
Top 10	33
Points	9596
Winnings	$37,779

Zipper Tops

The Holman-Moody Ford team bolted a top on Curtis Turner's Ford convertible late Saturday afternoon on Feb. 22, 1958, following the Daytona Beach Convertible race. Turner won the ragtop event, then drove the same car in Sunday's NASCAR Grand National race. NASCAR rules permitted the use of "zipper tops" for teams that wanted to use the same car in different divisions. Turner ran a close second to Paul Goldsmith in the NASCAR Grand National race on the Beach-Road course.

The Final Beach Race

In the final lap of the Feb. 23, 1958, Daytona Beach NASCAR Grand National event, #3 Paul Goldsmith nearly slid over the edge of the north turn. His vision obscured by wet sand and moisture from the ocean spray, Goldsmith found it difficult to see out of the window of his Smokey Yunick-prepared Pontiac. Windshield wipers were a standard piece of equipment on cars running the Daytona event, but Goldsmith's were inoperative, having blown back over the roof. Goldsmith's big lead evaporated on the final lap, but he still made it to the finish line just ahead of the hard-charging Curtis Turner to win the final race held on the storied course along the shoreline. A week later, Goldsmith quit the NASCAR tour and joined the rival USAC organization so he could get a shot at the Indianapolis 500. Goldsmith competed in five Indy 500s from '58 to '63, twice finishing in the top five. He later returned to NASCAR.

The 1958 Southern 500

The Sept. 1, 1958, Southern 500 at Darlington Raceway remains one of the most spectacular races on record. Three cars sailed out of the speedway, including Eddie Pagan's #45 Ford which blasted through the guardrail after blowing a tire on lap 137. Eddie Gray left the building on lap 160, and Jack Smith's #47 Pontiac bounced over the wall on lap 207. Miraculously, none of the drivers were injured. Fireball Roberts drove his #22 Chevrolet to a five-lap victory over runner-up Buck Baker. With the win, Roberts became the first driver to win three super-speedway races in a single year.

1958
NASCAR GRAND NATIONAL CHAMPION
Lee Petty

Old pro Lee Petty was a dominant force in 1958 NASCAR Grand National competition, leading the points standings after all but the season's first race.

Petty won seven of his 50 starts and finished 644 points ahead of runner-up Buck Baker. Petty finished out of the top 10 in only six races, and held a comfortable margin in the points race nearly the entire season. He took the lead for keeps with a sixth-place finish at Daytona. Rex White, who led after the first race, didn't make a concerted run at the title, competing in only 22 of the 51 races on the schedule.

Fireball Roberts drove in only 10 races, but he won six times and finished 11th in the final points standings. Roberts was also the leading money winner on the tour, pocketing $32,218.20.

Lee Petty
#42 Oldsmobile
Owner: Petty Engineering

Starts	50
Wins	7
Top 5	28
Top 10	44
Points	12,232
Winnings	$26,565

The First Daytona 500

Thirty-nine NASCAR Grand Nationals and 20 Convertibles started the inaugural Daytona 500 on Feb. 22, 1959. A packed house of 41,921 spectators jammed the grandstands and infield to watch the historic event. The race came down to a fight between #42 Lee Petty and #73 Johnny Beauchamp. Number 48 Joe Weatherly was two laps behind, but, without the help of radio communication, Weatherly wasn't sure if he was trailing the leaders. He continued to dice closely with Petty and Beauchamp throughout the final laps. Petty took the lead with four laps remaining, but Beauchamp pulled alongside Petty at the stripe. Beauchamp was initially declared the winner, but most observers with a clear view of the finish thought Petty had won. NASCAR and Daytona International Speedway president Bill France said the finish would be unofficial until photos and film footage could be studied. As film and still photographs came into NASCAR headquarters, more and more evidence built up to support Lee Petty as the winner. On Wednesday, Feb. 25, film arrived from the Hearst Metrotone News of the Week. The footage removed all doubt and Petty was declared the official winner, 61 hours after the inaugural Daytona 500 had ended.

Sweepstakes Races

At 18 select races from 1956 to '59, the NASCAR Grand National hardtops and Convertibles raced together in events called "Sweepstakes Races." Convertibles won six of these events. The 1959 Daytona 500 (below) revealed that the open-top cars were unstable in the buffeting winds of a superspeedway and about 10 mph slower than their more streamlined counterparts. With more superspeedways set to open and interest waning, '59 became the final full season for the NASCAR Convertible Division. Only 15 Convertible races were run in '59, plus eight Sweepstakes events that counted as points races for the Convertible circuit. Rex White won the final Sweepstakes race on Sept. 27, 1959, at Martinsville Speedway in a Chevrolet hardtop; Glen Wood finished second in a Ford Convertible. The '60 Daytona 500 was originally scheduled as a Sweepstakes event, but after only a handful of ragtops entered, Bill France elected to make it strictly a Grand National event. The hardtops and Convertibles never ran together again.

Richard Petty

Richard Petty, shown here in the sleeveless driver's "uniform" that was routine apparel in the late 1950s, was the third recipient of the Rookie of the Year award in 1959. Upon turning 21, Petty started nine races in 1958, then started 21 races and recorded nine top-10 finishes while driving Oldsmobiles and Plymouths from the Petty Enterprises shops in '59. Richard was probably ready for NASCAR competition by the time he was 18, but his father Lee prohibited him from competing until he was 21. In addition to his NASCAR Grand National activities in '59, Petty competed in a dozen NASCAR Convertible events, winning once and finishing fourth in the points standings.

Pettys vs. Bakers

A special match race between the Petty and Baker
families was added to the racing card at Hillsboro,
North Carolina's Orange Speedway on Sept. 20, 1959.
The younger generation of Richard Petty and Buddy
Baker started on the front row. Young Buddy, who was
at the wheel of Tom Pistone's powerful Ford Thunderbird,
won the 10-lap match race on the 0.9-mile dirt track.

1959

Lee Petty

Lee Petty became the first three-time winner of the NASCAR Grand National championship by dominating the 1959 season. Petty's victory in the inaugural Daytona 500 pushed him atop the standings, a perch he never relinquished. Petty finished 1830 points ahead of Cotton Owens in the final tally.

The 45-year-old Petty won other major events at North Wilkesboro, Atlanta, Martinsville, and Hillsboro. His 11 race wins more than doubled that of any other driver during the season.

Bob Welborn won the season's opening two races and led the early standings, but he concentrated more heavily on NASCAR's convertible circuit. Welborn competed in 28 of the 44 NASCAR Grand National races and finished 17th in the final points standings.

With his dominant season, Petty established an all-time NASCAR record by leading the points standings after 92 of the 95 races in 1958 and '59.

Lee Petty
#42 Oldsmobile
Owner: Petty Engineering

Starts	42
Wins	11
Top 5	27
Top 10	35
Points	11,792
Winnings	$49,219

the 1960s ▶▶

The King's First Victory

A crowd of 7489 witnessed history from the covered grandstands at Charlotte's Fairgrounds Speedway on Feb. 28, 1960. Lined up on the inside of the fourth row is young Richard Petty in the white #43 Plymouth. In his 35th start, Petty, with an assist from his father Lee, scored his first of 200 NASCAR Grand National wins. The elder Petty popped Rex White out of the way in the closing stages, allowing Richard to make the decisive pass. Richard had been flagged in first place in a July 1959 race at Atlanta, but his apparent victory was protested by second place finisher Lee Petty, who claimed he had lapped Richard. After studying the scorecards, NASCAR reversed the decision and awarded the win to Lee.

1960

NASCAR GRAND NATIONAL CHAMPION

Rex White

The pint-sized Rex White took the points lead in June and never looked back as he sped to his first NASCAR Grand National championship.

White grabbed first place in the standings in June following the inaugural World 600 at the new Charlotte Motor Speedway, where he finished sixth. He won six races in 40 starts and finished 3936 points ahead of runner-up Richard Petty.

Petty suffered a major setback when he was disqualified at Charlotte for making an improper entrance to pit road. Petty had finished fourth in the 600-miler, worth 3520 points, but when NASCAR disqualified him, he lost all those points. Petty won three times during the year, including his first career win at the old Charlotte Fairgrounds in February.

The points lead changed hands seven times among five different drivers. Jack Smith, Junior Johnson, and Bobby Johns also led the standings.

Rex White
#4, 16, 74 Chevy, Ford
Owners: Rex White,
L. D. Austin

Starts	48
Wins	14
Top 5	31
Top 10	39
Points	9272
Winnings	$34,076

Flight out of Daytona

Lee Petty and Johnny Beauchamp were involved in a horrifying last-lap crash in the second Twin 100-mile qualifying race for the 1961 Daytona 500. After Beauchamp's #73 Chevrolet snagged the rear bumper of Petty's #42 Plymouth, both cars broke through the guardrail and soared out of the speedway. Petty suffered multiple life-threatening injuries, while Beauchamp sustained less-serious head injuries. In a separate crash, Richard Petty also went over the wall, but his car remained on all four wheels and he walked away. The crashes left the Petty team unable to compete in the Daytona 500.

Curtis Turner and the Teamsters

By 1961, the NASCAR Grand National circuit had become a thriving business, and new modern speedways were being built from Florida to California. One of the new superspeedway projects, Charlotte Motor Speedway, was headed up by NASCAR racer Curtis Turner and short-track promoter Bruton Smith.

Construction costs greatly exceeded estimates for the 1½-mile speedway. Turner and Smith were booted out of the Charlotte Motor Speedway project in June 1961, the victims of a stormy board of directors meeting. Turner, in a last-ditch effort to regain control of the speedway, approached the Teamsters Union for a loan of more than $800,000. In return for the loan, Turner was asked to organize NASCAR drivers into a union called the Federation of Professional Athletes.

The purpose was to form a union of all professional drivers cutting across NASCAR, USAC, IMCA, and other boundaries. Targeted benefits were better purses, pension plans, more adequate insurance coverage, a scholarship fund for children of deceased members, and upgraded facilities for drivers at the speedways. A majority of NASCAR Grand National drivers joined up. What the Teamsters didn't point out to the drivers was their desire to get pari-mutuel gambling approved so America could bet on the results of the races.

On Aug. 8, Turner announced that a majority of the drivers on the NASCAR

Grand National Circuit had joined the Federation of Professional Athletes.

The proverbial mess hit the fan when Big Bill France heard the news.

"No known Teamster member can compete in a NASCAR race," France insisted. "And I'll use a pistol to enforce it." France flew to Winston-Salem, N.C., on Aug. 9 and spoke with the drivers. "Gentlemen, before I have this union stuffed down my throat, I will plow up my 2½-mile track in Daytona Beach and plant corn in the infield." France also told the drivers present that Curtis Turner, Tim Flock, and Fireball Roberts, three principle drivers who were recruiting members, "have been suspended for life for conduct detrimental to auto racing."

The NASCAR/Teamsters battle escalated to war within hours. Turner released a lengthy discourse detailing the urgent need to address the aforementioned concerns, plus some new ones, including a greater awareness of safety precautions.

France countered: "I am not quite sure yet if it's just plain foolishness or stupidity that makes these boys get associated with movements which can only hurt and degrade our sport and injure the people and organization that helped them grow. I do know that organized gambling would be bad for our sport. It would spill innocent blood on our racetracks. I will fight this to the end."

The first domino tumbled in favor of France on Aug. 11, when Fireball Roberts resigned from the Federation of Professional Athletes, questioning the motives of the FPA officers and recognizing the Teamsters as a threat. Roberts was reinstated, and other top-ranked NASCAR drivers followed in resigning from the FPA.

With virtually all of the drivers back in Bill France's fold, Curtis Turner and Tim Flock, the only two who held their positions in the union effort, weren't forgiven by Big Bill. The "life" suspensions were upheld.

Turner and Flock filed several lawsuits, plus a request for a temporary injunction. After the injunction was dismissed on Jan. 13, 1962, Turner's attorneys advised him to drop all suits against NASCAR. The clincher was that the Teamsters couldn't have loaned money to a company they were attempting to organize.

Turner and Bruton Smith lost control of the Charlotte Motor Speedway and it went into bankruptcy, but a new board of directors revived the speedway.

Following the Teamster episode, NASCAR formed a NASCAR Grand National Advisory Board to address the drivers' grievances. The panel was made up of two members each among drivers, NASCAR executives, car owners, and promoters.

France reinstated Curtis Turner in 1965, and he drove until '68. Tim Flock's career was winding down by '61, though, and he never competed in NASCAR again.

Basic Transportation

In the early 1960s, NASCAR race teams weren't the megadollar, professional operations run today. Instead of custom-built semi trailers, most of the NASCAR Grand National teams used flatbed trailers to haul their cars from track to track. All of the spare parts of Jimmy Pardue's

Chevrolet team were crammed into the back of a conventional Chevrolet pickup truck. With modest sponsorship from Fred Gaddy Leasing Co. in North Wilkesboro, Pardue was able to make 44 races in '61, finishing in the top 10 in 16 events. Pardue finished 11th in the final NASCAR Grand National points standings that year.

1961

Ned Jarrett

Ned Jarrett won only one race during the 1961 season, a 100-miler at Birmingham in June, but it was good enough to walk away with the NASCAR Grand National championship.

Jarrett and 1960 champion Rex White engaged in a tight duel throughout the summer. Jarrett took the points lead after the 34th race of the season at Columbia, S.C., and led the rest of the way. Jarrett finished 830 points ahead of White at the conclusion of the 52-race season.

White won seven races and logged 38 top-10 finishes in 47 starts, while Jarrett had 34 top-10 finishes in 46 starts. The points lead changed hands seven times among five drivers during the season.

Emanuel Zervakis placed third in the final standings. Nine-time winner Joe Weatherly was fourth, and two-time winner Fireball Roberts finished fifth.

Ned Jarrett
#11 Chevrolet, Ford
Owner: B.G. Holloway

Starts	46
Wins	1
Top 5	23
Top 10	34
Points	27,272
Winnings	$41,055

Requiem for a Convertible

The NASCAR Convertible cars made their final appearance in the May 12, 1962, Rebel 300 at Darlington Raceway. Nelson Stacy, driving the #29 Ford for the Holman-Moody team, went into the record books as the winner of the final ragtop race. Marvin Panch finished a close second in the #21 Wood Brothers Ford. Stacy was added to the Holman-Moody Ford team in 1961 and immediately clicked off a NASCAR Grand National victory in the Southern 500. In '62, Stacy won three races for Ford as Fred Lorenzen's teammate, capturing wins at Darlington, Charlotte, and Martinsville.

1962: Pontiacs on the Prowl

The 1957 factory withdrawal from auto racing, handed down by the Automobile Manufacturers Association, was loosely interpreted by each automaker. While Ford and Chrysler adhered to the strict "hands-off" policy, General Motors was more liberal with its assessment of the guidelines.

GM disguised its factory support of NASCAR racing by passing it off as an independent effort by automobile dealerships. Pontiac and Chevrolet dealership names adorned the sides of many NASCAR stockers in the early '60s.

Not surprisingly, Pontiac and Chevrolet dominated the 1962 NASCAR Grand National season, combining to win 36 of the 53 races. Pontiac drivers claimed most of the top honors, including Joe Weatherly's title run and Fireball Roberts' complete sweep of the Daytona Speedweek events. Roberts (opposite, top) was undefeated at Daytona in '62 in a Smokey Yunick-prepared Pontiac.

In the summer of 1962, Ford announced it was returning full force to NASCAR, thus side-stepping the 1957 AMA resolution. Ford, with millions to spend, represented a genuine threat to GM dominance.

The 1962 NASCAR Grand National campaign was the last year of GM dominance, until the landscape dramatically changed in the 1970s.

1962

NASCAR GRAND NATIONAL CHAMPION

Joe Weatherly

Joe Weatherly, in his second year driving Bud Moore's Pontiacs, won the 1962 NASCAR Grand National championship. Weatherly won nine races and posted 31 top-three finishes in 52 starts in his impressive drive to the title.

Weatherly took the points lead in late May following a runner-up finish in Charlotte's World 600 and sprinted to a 2396-point margin over Richard Petty. The Norfolk, Va., veteran won eight races on short tracks and one at Daytona. He only finished out of the top 10 in only seven of his 52 starts.

The points lead swapped hands five times among three drivers. Weatherly held the lead most of the way, relinquishing it to Jack Smith for two races in May. Petty won eight races, but was no match for Weatherly in the points race. Six-time winner Ned Jarrett placed third in the standings.

Joe Weatherly
#8 Pontiac
Owner: Bud Moore

Starts	52
Wins	9
Top 5	39
Top 10	45
Points	30,836
Winnings	$70,742

1963: Ford's Total Performance

In the early 1960s, Ford Motor Co. began an all-out assault on motorsports. Ford's "Total Performance" package would cost the automotive giant millions, but it would reap rewards far beyond the heavy expenditures.

In mid 1962, Ford withdrew from the 1957 AMA Resolution, which forbade the automakers from actively financing racing teams. The second half of the '62 NASCAR season was merely a tune-up for the onslaught of '63. Ford hit stride in '63, winning the first 500-miler of the year at Riverside, then making an impressive 1-2-3-4-5 sweep of the Daytona 500. Tiny Lund, driving the Wood Brothers #21 Ford, led the Ford charge at Daytona.

Other big superspeedway victories followed. Fred Lorenzen, at the controls of Ford's number-one NASCAR team, took his Holman-Moody Ford to six victories. Former Pontiac pilot Fireball Roberts joined the Holman-Moody Ford team in March, and promptly won at Bristol, Daytona, and Darlington.

Other top-ranked drivers left the sagging GM team to join Ford and Mercury. Joe Weatherly, Rex White, and Ned Jarrett were among the defectors.

Weatherly won the NASCAR Grand National title for the second consecutive season while driving Bud Moore's Mercury. Lorenzen shattered the all-time single-season earnings record. Lorenzen pocketed more than $120,000, and finished third in the final points standings despite running only about half the schedule. For the year, Ford products won 24 races, compared to just six in 1962.

**Bang! The big, tough Fords outlast all competition
...sweep Daytona's Firecracker 400**

Daytona Beach, July 6. Thirty-five of the country's finest cars took the starter's flag today in the annual Firecracker 400. Only 11 cars finished. That's how tough the race was.

Six out of nine Fords in the event were still going strong at the finish. That's how tough the 1963 Fords are.

**BIG YEAR FOR
FORD'S TOTAL PERFORMANCE**

Ford's domination of this 400-mile classic logs an unprecedented string of victories in stock car events, rallies and performance trials this spring—including a history-making five-car sweep of the Daytona 500 in February.

You need more than just a fast car to win events like these. Almost all the cars entered at Daytona had the speed to win. But, it takes total performance—the right combination of handling, braking, cornering, acceleration and absolute durability to stand up to the brutal demands of major stock car competitions.

Ford's total performance has been bred in open competition. Our cars are more durable, easier to handle, quieter and more comfortable because of things we have learned in competition at places like Daytona, Riverside, Atlanta, and the Pure Oil Performance Trials. What we have learned pays off for you every day in your kind of driving. Before you buy any new car, test-drive a solid, silent Super Torque Ford. Make this important discovery:

If it's built by Ford, it's built for performance—total performance!

FORD

1963

NASCAR GRAND NATIONAL CHAMPION

Joe Weatherly

Joe Weatherly authored the most unlikely championship run in NASCAR history in 1963, driving for nine different team owners. Weatherly's primary team, owned by Bud Moore, entered only major events, leaving Weatherly without a ride for most of the short-track races. Weatherly showed up at each track and borrowed a car to accumulate points.

Weatherly won three races and finished 2228 points ahead of 14-time winner Richard Petty. He took the lead in the standings for keeps following a fourth-place finish in the Charlotte World 600 in late May.

Weatherly's finishes in superspeedway races contributed greatly to his title run. Under NASCAR's points system, high-dollar events offered more points. Weatherly averaged an eighth-place finish in the 10 races on large tracks while Petty averaged 17th.

Fred Lorenzen, the first driver to win over $100,000 in a single season, finished third in points despite missing 26 of the year's 55 races.

Joe Weatherly
#8, 2, 05, 17, 36, 41, 57, 83, 88, 361
Pontiac, Mercury, Chrysler, Dodge, Plymouth
Owners: Bud Moore, Fred Harb, Pete Stewart, Major Melton, Cliff Stewart, Worth McMillion, Petty Engineering, Wade Younts, one team unknown

Starts	53
Wins	3
Top 5	20
Top 10	35
Points	33,398
Winnings	$74,623

1964: The Hemi Unleashed

By the end of the 1963 season, Ford had moved to the top rung of NASCAR's performance ladder. General Motors was in full retreat and Chrysler was looking to advance into the competitive ranks on the superspeedways.

During the '63 NASCAR Grand National campaign, Chrysler had an upgraded engine package, which helped the Petty Enterprises Plymouth team to win 19 races. Virtually all were on short tracks. Chrysler's efforts on the superspeedways were mediocre at best, largely due to a lack of aerodynamic bodies.

For 1964, Chrysler reworked the body design and dusted off the blueprints of a powerplant that had been in its bag of tricks since 1951—the hemispherical combustion engine, better known as the Hemi.

At Daytona in 1964, the MoPars ran circles around the Fords. Richard Petty qualified 20 mph faster than he had the previous year. The new streamlined Plymouth Belvederes and Dodge Coronets, with their potent Hemis, grabbed virtually every top honor at Daytona, including a 1-2-3 sweep in the 500-miler.

Fords won most of the short-track events, as well as many superspeedway races. At some venues, the Chryslers had too much power for their own good. For the season, Fords claimed 35 wins compared to Chrysler's 26. Although Ford won more races, Chrysler had made great strides, winning a much bigger portion of superspeedway races than in '63 and seven more races overall.

Lorenzen's Winning Streak

Fred Lorenzen experienced mechanical problems in the first four races of the 1964 NASCAR Grand National season, but then went on a tear after the Daytona 500. He drove his #28 Holman-Moody Ford to victories in five consecutive starts at Bristol, Atlanta, North Wilkesboro, Martinsville, and Darlington. After the Darlington race, Lorenzen's crew chief Herb Nab was fired by team owner John Holman for refusing to obey orders. Nab didn't tell Lorenzen to come in for a late pit stop. The strategy worked as Lorenzen won, but Holman didn't like being ignored. Nab was rehired two days later. Of the 1953 laps during the five-race stretch, Lorenzen led 1679 of them. It remains one of the most dominating performances in NASCAR history.

A Tragic Year

The 1964 NASCAR Grand National season remains the most tragic on record. Joe Weatherly, two-time defending NASCAR Grand National champion, lost his life in January at Riverside after crashing into a concrete wall. NASCAR icon Fireball Roberts suffered burns in Charlotte's May 24 World 600 and succumbed to those injuries in July. Jimmy Pardue, who ranked fourth in points at the time, died in a tire-test crash at Charlotte Motor Speedway on Sept. 20. NASCAR responded to the tragedies by enacting rules to make the cars slower for the 1965 season.

1964

Richard Petty

Richard Petty won nine races, including his first on a superspeedway, and ran away with the 1964 NASCAR Grand National championship. Petty finished a staggering 5302 points ahead of runner-up Ned Jarrett, who won 15 races.

Petty took the points lead after the 25th race of the season with a runner-up finish in the World 600 at Charlotte. He continued to pad his lead during the balance of the 62-race season.

Two-time defending champion Joe Weatherly led the standings early in the season. He was the top points man entering the Riverside 500 in January (the '64 season started in November '63), but lost his life in a crash late in the event.

The points lead changed hands six times among four drivers in '64. Marvin Panch led from late February through late May, but fell to 10th in the final tally.

David Pearson made his first concentrated effort for the championship and finished third with eight wins. Sophomore Billy Wade came in fourth and Jimmy Pardue, who was fatally injured in September, still placed fifth in the points race.

Richard Petty
#43, 42, 41 Plymouth
Owner: Petty Engineering

Starts	61
Wins	9
Top 5	37
Top 10	43
Points	40,252
Winnings	$114,771

1965: Ford's Hollow Victories

The Ford nameplate won 33 of the first 34 NASCAR Grand National races in the 1965 season. From Feb. 12 through July 25, Ford went undefeated, winning a record 32 consecutive Grand Nationals. Both remain all-time records.

While Ford was piling win upon win, statisticians were busy placing asterisks next to the lofty numbers. None of the early season races offered a full compliment of rival factory teams. General Motors was gone, and Chrysler was sitting on the sidelines in an effective boycott. Ford was winning with almost no competition.

NASCAR's new regulations for 1965 had outlawed the Chrysler Hemi engine and the models Plymouth and Dodge teams had fielded in '64. With no eligible cars, Chrysler boycotted—and Ford cleaned house. Sidelined, Chrysler drivers turned to other pursuits. Richard Petty tried his hand at drag racing (opposite page, center). LeeRoy Yarbrough made a special run against the clock at Daytona in a supercharged Dodge Coronet (opposite, top left). Yarbrough turned a lap of 181.818 mph, establishing a new closed-course record for stock cars. Meanwhile, Ford drivers cleaned up: Dick Hutcherson (opposite, top right) won nine races, Junior Johnson (opposite, bottom) won 13, and Ned Jarrett won 13 races and the 1965 NASCAR Grand National Championship.

Chrysler's pull-out had a telling effect. Speedway owners were taking it on the chin as trackside attendance suffered. NASCAR heard the complaints and, by July, allowed the Chrysler teams to return, but only on short tracks.

Eventually, NASCAR lifted the restrictions, and the Hemi-powered Plymouths and Dodges returned. Curiously, Ford won the final six races of the season, and all but one had a full compliment of Chrysler teams. Ford won 48 of the 55 races in 1965, a record .872 winning percentage that may never be challenged.

127

Yarborough Takes Flight

Cale Yarborough's Ford sails over the Darlington Raceway guardrail after tangling with Sam McQuagg's #24 Ford on the 119th lap of the Sept. 6, 1965, Southern 500. Yarborough tried to make a daring pass on leader McQuagg, but their fenders touched and Yarborough's Ford went airborne. The car came to rest against a telephone pole outside the track and Yarborough was uninjured.

"I knew I was in trouble when I saw grass, because I know there ain't no grass on a racetrack."
—Cale Yarborough

Dynamic Duel

One of the most sensational duels in NASCAR history came in the late laps of the Oct. 17, 1965, National 400 at Charlotte Motor Speedway. The Fords of #29 Dick Hutcherson, #28 Fred Lorenzen, and #41 Curtis Turner (who had returned from suspension midseason) battled three-abreast for the lead, with A. J. Foyt also in the mix. With six laps to go, Foyt spun as he attempted to overtake Lorenzen for the lead. Hutcherson had to take evasive action and Turner was forced into a spin to avoid hitting Foyt. Lorenzen scampered home first, with Hutcherson close behind; Turner finished third. Ned Jarrett avoided the melee to come home fourth and clinch his second NASCAR Grand National Championship.

1965

NASCAR GRAND NATIONAL CHAMPION

Ned Jarrett

Veteran Ned Jarrett prevailed in a season-long struggle with rookie driver Dick Hutcherson to capture his second NASCAR Grand National championship. Jarrett and Hutcherson traded the points lead five times during the season.

Jarrett's quest for a second title was in jeopardy when he injured his back in a race at Greenville, S.C., in June. With the aid of a back brace, Jarrett continued and managed to overtake Hutcherson in the 34th race of the season at Bristol. Jarrett won 13 races, while Hutcherson set an all-time record for a freshman by winning nine events. Hutcherson led the standings after 13 races, another rookie record.

The points lead changed hands six times among four drivers during the 55-race campaign. Junior Johnson and Darel Dieringer led briefly during the early stages. Dieringer placed third in the final tally, ahead of G.C. Spencer and Marvin Panch.

Ned Jarrett
#11, 25 Ford
Owners: Bondy Long, Jabe Thomas

Starts	54
Wins	13
Top 5	42
Top 10	45
Points	38,824
Winnings	$93,624

1966: The Hemi Returns, Ford Boycotts

The 1965 Chrysler boycott shook the foundation of NASCAR racing, and everyone involved suffered. All the Ford and Chrysler factory teams were on hand for the '66 Daytona 500 and all seemed well, but controversy struck again after only a few races. Ford was displeased that NASCAR had failed to approve its new single-overhead cam engine for competition. NASCAR said the new engine had limited availability, wasn't available to the motoring public, and was therefore ineligible.

In response, Ford boycotted NASCAR in the spring of 1966. The move left a parade of Plymouth and Dodge products to pluck all the top prizes.

Although NASCAR made no public admission, the rule book became flexible in the summer of '66. NASCAR may have let some rules slide to maintain trackside attendance. Junior Johnson showed up at Atlanta with a customized, chopped, and lowered contraption he called a Ford Galaxie. The media dubbed it the "Yellow Banana." Smokey Yunick built a Chevrolet Chevelle that had, among its creative elements, spoilers sprouting from the roof and off-centered wheels.

The Johnson and Yunick cars passed inspection. NASCAR may have allowed them to compete to generate interest, but the sanctioning body's credibility took a hit. By the end of the year, though, loopholes in the rule book were closed and Ford and Chrysler were battling on the track instead of the picket line.

"I ain't never seen anybody who could drive a banana at 150 mile 'n hour."

—Anonymous

Chrysler Corp. cars won 34 of the 49 races in 1966. Opposite: Jim Paschal takes the checkered flag at North Wilkesboro on April 17 in a Plymouth. Without factory support, Ford and GM crew chiefs had to improvise. The Junior Johnson-built "Yellow Banana" (above) featured a chopped top, a lowered stance, and a rear end that kicked up at the back. Smokey Yunick entered a Chevelle (left) with an altered wheelbase and a roof spoiler.

1966
David Pearson

David Pearson took the lead in the 1966 NASCAR Grand National points standings in the second event of the season and sprinted to an easy win over rookie James Hylton. Pearson finished 1950 points ahead of Hylton in the final tally.

Hylton's runner-up effort marked the second straight season a rookie driver finished second in the NASCAR Grand National points race.

Pearson, driving Cotton Owens' Dodge, scored 15 victories during the season. Hylton failed to post any wins, but was able to finish 32 of his 41 starts in the top 10. Pearson survived one close call during the championship chase. His car was ruled out of the 400-miler at Atlanta in August when NASCAR officials determined it didn't conform to specifications. Despite sitting out of the race, Pearson had enough cushion in the points to maintain his lead.

David Pearson
#6 Dodge
Owner: Cotton Owens

Starts	42
Wins	15
Top 5	26
Top 10	33
Points	35,638
Winnings	$78,193

Breakin' 180

Curtis Turner became the first driver to surpass 180 mph on an official qualifying run in 1967 Daytona 500 time trials. Turner's #13 Smokey Yunick Chevelle was clocked at 180.831 mph, earning the pole position. It was a controversial achievement for two reasons. First, it meant an unsponsored GM car had beaten the Ford and Chrysler factory entries. Second, the car was roughly ⅞ scale. An engine failure in the final 100 miles put Turner out of the Daytona 500.

Lorenzen's Last Win

Fred Lorenzen's 26th and final NASCAR Grand National victory came in the second Twin 100-miler at Daytona on Feb. 24, 1967. Lorenzen went the distance without a pit stop, the first driver to run nonstop in the qualifying race. NASCAR tacked on an additional 25 miles in subsequent years so teams would have to pit at least once during the Twin qualifying races. Lorenzen went on to finish second in the Daytona 500, but made only two more starts before suddenly retiring from competition at age 32. The Elmhurst, Ill., driver cited ulcers and a weight loss for the spur-of-the-moment decision. He played the stock market and remained on the sidelines until May 1970, when the itch returned and he made a comeback

attempt. Although he ran up front in a number of races, some of his competitive edge had been lost. By the fall of '72, Lorenzen bowed out of NASCAR for the final time.

**FRED LORENZEN
NASCAR
Grand National
Career Record
1956, 1960-67,
1970-72**
Starts: 158
Wins: 26
Top 5s: 75
Top 10s: 84
Poles: 33
Career Winnings:
$496,574

Andretti Wins Daytona 500

Mario Andretti dominated the Feb. 26, 1967, Daytona 500, leading 112 of 200 laps in his #11 Holman-Moody Ford on his way to victory. It was only his seventh career NASCAR Grand National start. Andretti never came close to winning another NASCAR event.

Body Templates

NASCAR began using body templates at the midpoint of the 1967 Grand National season. Innovative mechanics were getting downsized versions of full-size automobiles through the inspection procedure. Templates measured the body and contour of cars to make sure they conformed to stock guidelines. Below, inspectors measure a stock car. At the right, Armond Holley's Chevrolet

goes through the ritual prior to the July 4 Firecracker 400 at Daytona International Speedway. Of the 50 entries for the event, 49 initially failed inspection. Bud Moore's Mercury was the only car to pass the first time.

1967

Richard Petty

Richard Petty rewrote the record book in 1967, winning 27 races in 46 starts. The newly crowned "king" of stock car racing also won 10 races in a row. The 27 wins and 10-race streak set records that may never be matched.

Despite his thorough domination, Petty didn't grab the points lead until his 11th win of the season at Rockingham in late June. Winless James Hylton held the lead for six months due to consistency. Petty hit stride in the second half of the season, and sprinted to a 6028-point cushion over Hylton by the end of the 49-race schedule. Dick Hutcherson finished third in points in his final season as a driver. Up-and-coming driver Bobby Allison placed fourth.

Petty also became the all-time NASCAR victory leader, passing his father Lee by winning on May 13 at Darlington. It was the 55th triumph of Petty's career. And, with his 19th victory of the year, Petty surpassed the record of 18 wins set by Tim Flock (right) in 1955.

Richard Petty
#43 Plymouth
Owner: Petty Engineering

Starts	46
Wins	27
Top 5	38
Top 10	40
Points	942,472
Winnings	$150,196

1968

NASCAR GRAND NATIONAL CHAMPION
David Pearson

Torino WINS Rebel 400

**Torino—
Success Car '68
The record speaks for itself**

- May 11, 1968—Torino takes Rebel 400 at Darlington, S.C.—widens its lead in the NASCAR Manufacturer's Championship race.
- May 5, 1968—Torino double-header—wins Yankee 250 at Indianapolis and the Fireball 300 at Weaverville, N.C.
- April 21, 1968—Torino wins Gwyn Staley Memorial 250 at Wilkesboro, N.C.
- March 24, 1968—Torino takes the Richmond 250.
- March 17, 1968—Torino wins Southeastern 500 at Bristol, Tenn.
- February 2, 1968—Torino named Official Pace Car for the Indianapolis 500.
- January 21, 1968—Torino starts the season, taking the first 5 places in the Riverside 500.

Big Savings now at your Ford Dealer's SEE-THE-LIGHT Sale!

Davavid Pearson and Bobby Isaac engaged in a ferocious duel for the 1968 NASCAR Grand National championship before Pearson pulled away in the closing months. It was Pearson's second title.

Pearson won 16 races en route to the championship, while Isaac won three times. Pearson took the lead from Isaac after winning the Aug. 8 event at Columbia, S.C. Driving Holman-Moody Fords, Pearson survived two disqualifications, but still beat Isaac by 126 points.

NASCAR instituted a new points system for 1968, with 150 points available to the winner in races of 400 miles or more, 100 points for major short-track events, and 50 points for small short-track races.

Richard Petty, who tied Pearson with the most wins at 16, finished a distant third in the standings. Clyde Lynn came home fourth, and John Sears rounded out the season's top five.

David Pearson
#17, 84 Ford
Owners: Holman-Moody,
Roy Trantham

Starts	48
Wins	16
Top 5	36
Top 10	38
Points	3499
Winnings	$133,064

Petty Switches to Ford

After a 1968 season that produced only one superspeedway win in his Plymouth Roadrunner, Richard Petty requested that Chrysler officials shift him to the more aerodynamic Dodge for the 1969 NASCAR Grand National campaign. Chrysler balked, indicating they wanted to keep him in the Plymouth nameplate. In a shocking decision, Petty bailed out of the Chrysler camp entirely and joined the powerful Ford team. The King of NASCAR racing won his first start in a Ford at Riverside and went on to score eight other wins in the Torino Talladega.

Aerodynamic Push

Ford Motor Co. introduced sloped nose extensions on its Ford Torinos and Mercury Cyclones in 1969 in an effort to lengthen their advantage over Chrysler's products. Combined with the new 429-cid Blue Crescent engine, the extensions provided a definite advantage over the conventional Dodge Chargers, particularly on super-speedways. Ford didn't lose on a superspeedway until Sept. 14, when the Dodge Charger Daytona made its first appearance in NASCAR. Chrysler executives realized they needed to explore the reaches of aerodynamics to compete with the

powerful Fords, and did so by adding a pointed nose and a high wing to its Dodge Charger. The Daytona was unveiled at the inaugural Talladega 500. Although the race was marred by a drivers' boycott, Richard Brickhouse drove his Dodge Daytona to a first-place finish in its maiden voyage in high-speed competition.

Trouble at Talladega

NASCAR president Bill France, who had opened Daytona International Speedway in 1959, was the mastermind behind an even bigger speedway project in '69. Talladega's Alabama International Motor Speedway would be the world's fastest closed course. Shakedown runs indicated the 200-mph barrier was within reach.

As the speedway was nearing completion, dissent grew within the driver ranks. In August 1969, the drivers held a secret meeting in Ann Arbor, Mich., to discuss concerns about driver facilities at the speedways, the lack of prize money in the face of rising expenses, and the alarming speeds at Talladega.

The 11 drivers at the meeting formed the Professional Drivers Association with Richard Petty as president. Less than two weeks before the inaugural Talladega 500, most of the NASCAR Grand National regulars had become PDA members.

When teams arrived at Talladega and began their initial practice runs, it was apparent that the tire companies hadn't had enough time to develop a tire to withstand speeds of nearly 200 mph. Tires were shredding apart at speeds over 190.

Impromptu meetings (below) took place frequently during the race weekend as drivers considered a boycott. The PDA asked Bill France to postpone the race until better tires could be produced. France refused, telling the drivers to slow down, then donned a helmet and took a 1969 Ford out for a practice run (opposite, top). He ran 175 mph, which France proudly exclaimed, "is a new world record for a 59-year-old man." France filed an entry for the race, hoping to gain admission

to the PDA's private meetings. The PDA prevented France from joining the talks.

After a series of tests, Firestone pulled its tires out of the race. France talked Goodyear into staying, but the tire giant said it wouldn't mount tires on any car that qualified above 190 mph.

Less than 24 hours before the start of the first Talladega 500, most of the drivers pulled out of the race. It was the first official drivers boycott in NASCAR history.

Sophomore Richard Brickhouse was offered a ride by Ray Nichels. Brickhouse had been a PDA member but withdrew on Sept. 14, the morning of the Talladega 500. He would drive the #99 Dodge Charger Daytona (below), one of two aerodynamic Dodges that debuted at Talladega (Bobby Isaac drove the other, the #71 car).

Thirteen NASCAR Grand National drivers competed against 23 drivers from the NASCAR Grand Touring ponycar division. Several mandated caution flags kept tire temperatures in check. Brickhouse won the race, which was run without a crash.

The PDA drivers returned to the speedways after Talladega, albeit with considerable tension. The PDA's concerns were heard, though, and by 1970, race tires were able to handle NASCAR's increasing speeds.

1969
David Pearson

148

David Pearson racked up his third NASCAR Grand National championship in 1969, taking the points lead from Richard Petty in April and holding it for the remainder of the 54-race season.

Petty's bid for a third championship was derailed in May when he missed two races due to broken ribs suffered in a crash at Asheville-Weaverville Speedway.

Pearson's third NASCAR title came in only his fourth concentrated attempt at the largest plum of the annual NASCAR Grand National campaign. He finished third in 1964 during his first full-season run, and won in '66, '68, and '69.

Bobby Isaac was the most prolific winner in 1969, taking the checkered flag 17 times. He finished sixth in the final standings.

David Pearson
#17 Ford
Owners: Holman-Moody

Starts	51
Wins	11
Top 5	42
Top 10	44
Points	4170
Winnings	$229,760

Petty Returns to Plymouth

Following a one-year stint with Ford, Richard Petty was lured back into the Plymouth fold in 1970 with the development of the new winged Plymouth Super-bird. Chrysler had to pro-duce more than 1500 of the new models (1920 were built) to gain acceptance from NASCAR to enter Grand National competi-tion. Prior to '70, only 500 factory examples were required to make a car eligible. Chrysler officials determined it was neces-sary to build the increased number of units to reac-quire the services of NASCAR's leading driver.

The Fastest Man on Four Wheels

On March 24, 1970, Buddy Baker took a royal blue Dodge Daytona to Talladega's Alabama International Motor Speedway for a special world record attempt on a closed circuit. In an officially timed run, Baker became the first driver to surpass the magic 200-mph barrier on a closed oval. His best lap was 200.447 mph, earning him the nickname "The Fastest Man on Four Wheels." Bobby Isaac beat the record seven months later, on Nov. 24, with a run of 201.104 mph.

1970

NASCAR GRAND NATIONAL CHAMPION
Bobby Isaac

B obby Isaac overtook James Hylton in late August and won the 1970 NASCAR Grand National championship. It was the most competitive title chase in NASCAR history. A total of seven drivers swapped the points lead on 12 occasions during the 48-race campaign, a record that still stands.

Isaac moved to the front with a runner-up finish in the Talladega 500 and stayed atop the standings for the final 14 events. Hylton lost his fading hopes for the title when he crashed at Charlotte in October. Bobby Allison surged past Hylton to capture second place in the final standings, 51 points behind Isaac.

For the second straight year, Richard Petty's hopes for a third title were dashed when he missed races due to injury. Petty managed to finish fourth overall.

The seven drivers who led the points race at one point were Isaac, Hylton, Allison, Petty, Dave Marcis, Neil Castles, and LeeRoy Yarbrough.

Bobby Isaac
#71 Dodge
Owner: Nord Krauskopf
Sponsor: K&K Insurance

Starts	47
Wins	11
Top 5	32
Top 10	38
Points	3911
Winnings	$199,600

1971: A Season of Change

After the 1970 Grand National campaign, NASCAR was somewhat unsettled. The automotive factories and their unlimited gravy train of sponsorship dollars and technical guidance were retreating. Ford had dropped out of racing entirely and the Chrysler contingent was reduced to two cars fielded by Petty Enterprises.

Without the surplus of factory parts at economical costs, the small-time privateers found themselves scrambling to field teams. The outlook was bleak, until R.J. Reynolds stepped into the picture in December 1970.

Congress had removed all tobacco advertising from network television in 1971, leaving the tobacco companies in search of a new venue to publicize their products. Auto racing became fertile ground. Viceroy backed the United States Auto Club's Indy Car circuit, while R.J. Reynolds and its Winston brand sank funds into NASCAR, changing the series' name to NASCAR Winston Cup Grand National.

Winston came to the rescue at the most opportune time, putting $100,000 into

NASCAR's championship points fund and supplying advertising for promoters who staged Grand National races of 250 miles or more. Winston's plunge into NASCAR stock car racing might have saved the series.

The 1971 season was marred by a number of controversial incidents. The newly introduced restrictor plates were different for each type of car/engine combination, drawing the ire of many drivers. The streamlined Plymouth Superbird and Dodge Daytona were limited to 305 cubic-inch displacements, basically legislating them out of the sport. Starting fields were dwindling, so NASCAR made a dramatic rule change to incorporate the Grand American division cars with the Grand Nationals in short-track races. Some promoters balked, refusing to comply with NASCAR's new rules. A number of teams boycotted in protest, while others withdrew due to lack of operating funds. It was a forgettable campaign.

Due to rules changes, the final appearance of Chrysler Corp.'s winged cars was Dick Brooks' run (opposite) at the 1971 Daytona 500. Defending champion Bobby Isaac (left) ran a limited schedule because of team owner Nord Krauskopf's dispute with NASCAR over restrictor-plate rules. With fields dwindling, NASCAR Grand American cars were permitted to run with the Grand Nationals in select races. Bobby Allison won the opening mixed-field event in Melvin Joseph's Coca-Cola-sponsored #49 Ford Mustang (below).

Underdog Chevy

With attendance sagging at most of the NASCAR tracks in 1971, Charlotte Motor Speedway general manager Richard Howard formed a Chevrolet team with Junior Johnson as manager and Charlie Glotzbach at the controls. Chevrolet hadn't been seriously competitive since it halted factory support in '63, and with the restrictor plates choking off the beefy Chrysler and Ford engines, the time was ripe for a competitive Chevrolet to return to NASCAR. Howard thought the return of both Chevrolet and Johnson to NASCAR competition would bring back the fans. He was right. Glotzbach won the pole for the May 30 World 600, and the seats were filled to near capacity. Glotzbach led often and ran with the leaders until he crashed just past the midway point. Glotzbach and relief driver Friday Hassler piloted the #3 Chevrolet to victory in the July 11 Volunteer 500 at Bristol International Speedway. In the lone win for the new Chevy team, Glotzbach and Hassler scored a three-lap victory in a caution-free event. It remains the only NASCAR Cup Series race in Bristol history without a caution flag.

1971
Richard Petty

Richard Petty won 21 races in 46 starts and breezed to his third NASCAR Cup Series championship. The "Randleman Rocket" assumed command of the points chase after the eighth race of the season at Hickory, N.C., in March, and never trailed again. He finished 364 points ahead of runner-up James Hylton.

Hylton, Bobby Allison, Benny Parsons, and Bobby Isaac jockeyed for the points lead early in the season before Petty set sail. Petty posted 38 top-five finishes in 46 starts to thoroughly dominate the title chase.

Allison, who joined the Holman-Moody team in May, won 11 races and finished fourth in the standings. He started 42 of the 48 races, but was never was able to challenge Petty for the points lead.

Only two drivers that finished in the top 10 won races during the campaign.

Richard Petty
#43 Plymouth
Owner: Petty Enterprises

Starts	46
Wins	21
Top 5	38
Top 10	41
Points	4435
Winnings	$351,071

Bill France, Jr., Takes Over

On Jan. 11, 1972, NASCAR founder Bill France stepped down as president of NASCAR and turned the reins over to his son, Bill France, Jr. (center, shown with Harry Hyde, left, and Bobby Isaac). "I am sure that NASCAR will continue its dynamic leadership in the sport of automobile racing," said the senior France. Prior to stepping down, however, the elder France set the circuit in order for the future. At title sponsor Winston's request, he eliminated all races under 250 miles, cutting the number of events from 48 to 31.

Foyt Wins Daytona

Tough Texan A. J. Foyt was signed to drive the #21 Wood Brothers Purolator Mercury in the early portion of the 1972 NASCAR Cup Series season. Foyt dominated the Feb. 20 Daytona 500, leading all but 33 laps and finishing nearly five miles ahead of runner-up Charlie Glotzbach. Full factory participation was missing in '72, and prerace experts noted that only five cars had a real shot at winning the race. Third-place Jim Vandiver finished six laps behind the leader, and 10th-place Vic Elford was more than 40 miles behind Foyt when the checkered flag fell. Foyt was unchallenged for the final 300 miles, and he became the second USAC Indy Car driver to pluck NASCAR's sweetest plum in the last six years. No visiting driver from another sanctioning body has won the Daytona 500 since.

NASCAR
Rookie Driver
Handbook

NASCAR ROOKIE DRIVER HANDBOOK

prepared by
UNION 76 DARLINGTON RECORD CLUB

NASCAR ROOKIE DRIVER HANDBOOK prepared by UNION 76-DARLINGTON RECORD CLUB

This handbook has been published to impress new NASCAR drivers with the strenuous physical, mental and technical requirements of the sport and vocation in which they are about to engage. The safety requirements and procedures covered in the handbook are based on the recommendations and experience of successful professional NASCAR champion drivers and veteran race officials. They are intended for the improvement and well-being of all drivers competing at not only Darlington International Raceway, but all speedways.

The Union 76-Darlington Record Club is one of the most exclusive clubs in the sport of stock car racing. To be eligible, a driver must be the fastest qualifier for the Southern 500 for his make of car for that year. Naturally, one man can be the fastest qualifier for a make of car for years, thus limiting the membership of the club. When a driver qualifies and

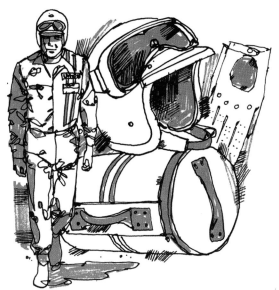

Freshman drivers on NASCAR's Cup Series were issued the NASCAR Rookie Driver Handbook when they checked into Darlington Raceway in preparation for the Sept. 4, 1972, Southern 500. The 16-page pocket-size guide offered guidelines on television and radio interviews, a dress code, and sponsor courtesy, stating, "Don't hesitate to mention the company's name if at all possible." The booklet also stressed the importance of physical fitness and gave tips for speaking to high school assemblies.

Petty-Allison Battles

One of the most thrilling moments in NASCAR history came during the final laps of the Oct. 1, 1972, race at North Wilkesboro Speedway. Richard Petty and Bobby Allison rekindled their ongoing feud, which dated back to 1967. The final five laps featured an epic slugfest between the two leading drivers. Allison led Petty under the white flag (this page), but Petty passed Allison after both cars hit the wall on the final lap and Petty won the final sprint to the finish line. Petty was attacked by a drunk fan in victory lane after the race, but order was restored when Richard's brother Maurice smacked the fan on the head with Richard's helmet.

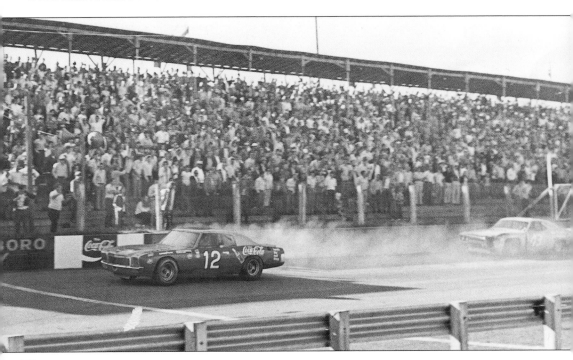

"He could have put me in the boondocks. There's not going to be any more trouble until he hurts me."
—Richard Petty

"He had to wreck me in order to win, and that's what he did. I had so much smoke in my car, I could hardly see."
—Bobby Allison

Vs

1972

Richard Petty

Richard Petty drove his Plymouths and Dodges to a record-setting fourth NASCAR Cup Series championship, leading in points for most of the season.

A new points system was introduced, which awarded points per lap completed. This system prevented Petty from taking the points lead until the 11th race of the season at Talladega. Petty had finished higher than James Hylton in nine of the first 10 races, including four wins, but Hylton maintained the points lead due to more laps completed. When Hylton was involved in a crash at Talladega, Petty claimed the lead, which he held for the balance of the season.

Petty won eight races and finished 127.9 points in front of runner-up Bobby Allison, who won 10 events. Hylton scored the first superspeedway victory of his career and finished third in the final standings.

Petty, Hylton, and Allison swapped the points lead six times during the season.

Richard Petty
#43 Plymouth, Dodge
Owner: Petty Enterprises
Sponsor: STP

Starts	31
Wins	8
Top 5	25
Top 10	28
Points	8701.40
Winnings	$339,405

"They wanted to fill up the track with those extra cars. They filled it up alright— all over the backstretch."
—Bobby Allison

Wreck-Filled Race

The backstretch of Talladega's Alabama International Motor Speedway is littered with wrecked cars and debris following a 21-car crash in the May 6 1973, Winston 500. The accident, which occurred on the 11th lap, took out 19 cars. The caution flag was out for more than 25 laps while safety crews cleaned up the mess. Many of the drivers blamed the huge crash on the 60-car starting field, the most cars to start a NASCAR Cup Series race in 13 years. The left side of Wendell Scott's #34 Mercury was sheared off in the crash. Scott escaped, but three broken ribs, lacerations, and a fractured pelvis put him on the mend for most of the season. Only 26 cars were running at the end of the race, which David Pearson won by more than a lap over runner-up Bobby Allison.

Unsponsored Upset

Dick Brooks' #22 Plymouth leads the charge off the fourth turn in the Aug. 12, 1973, Talladega 500. Brooks took the lead with seven laps remaining and motored home first in a stunning upset. Driving the unsponsored Crawford Brothers Plymouth, Brooks overcame a pit-road accident, overheating problems, and long pit stops by a ragtag crew. "I expected it to blow any minute. It wasn't until the last five laps that I realized I could win if the thing held together," said a joyous Brooks after the race. It was the final NASCAR Cup Series victory for the Plymouth nameplate.

Earnhardt Passes Away

NASCAR short-track icon Ralph Earnhardt, the 1956 Sportsman Division champion, suffered a heart attack and passed away on Sept. 26, 1973, at the age of 45. The elder Earnhardt was still active on short tracks at the time of his death. Between 1956 and '64, Earnhardt made 51 starts on the NASCAR Grand National tour, posting six top five and 10 top-10 finishes, but no wins.

Part-Time Domination

David Pearson enjoyed a record-wrecking year in 1973. Driving the Wood Brothers '71 Mercury, Pearson won 10 of 15 starts on superspeedways, and 11 of 18 for the season. During a 10-race stretch from March through August 1973, Pearson won nine races and finished second in the other event. Pearson won 14 of his first 22 starts with the Wood Brothers, including 13 on superspeedways. It was one of the most dominating performances in NASCAR's modern era.

David Pearson
1973 Record
#21 Mercury
Owner: Wood Brothers
Sponsor: Purolator

Season Rank	13th
Starts	18
Wins	11
Top 5	14
Top 10	14
Points	5382
Winnings	$228,408

173

1973

Benny Parsons

Benny Parsons, driving the unsponsored L.G. DeWitt Chevrolet, pulled a major upset by winning the 1973 NASCAR Cup Series championship despite only winning one race.

Parsons took the points lead with a third-place finish at Talladega in early May and never gave up the lead. He held off a late rally by Cale Yarborough to win by only 67.15 points.

Under NASCAR's points system, which awarded points per lap completed, Parsons was unaware of what position he would have to finish in at the finale at Rockingham to seal the championship. Parsons crashed early, but his team was able to make miraculous repairs to get him back into the race and complete enough laps to wrap up the 1973 title.

Five drivers had a mathematical chance to win the championship entering the final event of the 28-race season. Winless drivers Cecil Gordon and James Hylton finished third and fourth, while six-time winner Richard Petty placed fifth in the final standings.

Benny Parsons
#72 Chevrolet
Owner: L.G. DeWitt

Starts	28
Wins	1
Top 5	15
Top 10	21
Points	7173
Winnings	$182,321

1974
NASCAR CUP SERIES CHAMPION
Richard Petty

NASCAR changed its points system for 1974, and it proved to be the most confusing method ever used. Fractions of points were multiplied and remultiplied after each race. The concept was to award points in direct relation to money won.

Under the system, the 1-2 finishers in the rich Daytona 500 were virtually assured of a 1-2 finish in the final tally. Richard Petty and Cale Yarborough finished first and second at Daytona and ranked 1-2 in the final standings. All drama for the points chase ended in February. Petty and Yarborough had their Daytona points added to their point total after each event, making it virtually impossible for anyone to overtake them.

Petty accumulated 5037.75 points, compared to Yarborough's runner-up total of 4470.30. David Pearson finished third with 2389.25 points. Thankfully, the system was changed after only one year.

Richard Petty
#43 Dodge
Owner: Petty Enterprises
Sponsor: STP

Starts	30
Wins	10
Top 5	22
Top 10	22
Points	5037
Winnings	$432,019

Riverside

From 1970 to '81, the first race of the NASCAR Cup Series season was held at California's Riverside International Raceway. Here, Bobby Allison's Matador snakes its way through the legendary road course's "esses" on the way to victory in the 1975 season opener. Allison was the class of the field in the Winston Western 500, leading all but 18 of the 191 laps. Richard Petty, shown chasing Allison, fell out of contention when he backed into the wall on the 33rd lap. Petty lost 19 laps in the pits while repairs were made to his Dodge, but he still managed to finish seventh.

Earnhardt's First Start

Dale Earnhardt made his NASCAR Cup Series debut in the May 25, 1975, World 600 at Charlotte Motor Speedway. Driving the #8 Dodge Charger owned and maintained by independent driver Ed Negre, Earnhardt qualified third on the grid. He completed 355 of the 400 laps and finished 22nd. It was his only start this year. Earnhardt made two more starts in 1976, one in '77, and five in '78, before catching his big break with Osterlund Racing and earning Rookie of the Year honors in '79.

1975
Richard Petty

NASCAR instituted a new points system in 1975. It was the first time in history that every race on the NASCAR Cup Series schedule carried an equal point value.

Richard Petty won his sixth championship by a whopping 722 points over Dave Marcis. Petty took the points lead from Bobby Allison in the season's third race and never trailed

The new points system drew mixed reviews. While it was designed to encourage more teams to commit to running the full schedule, many observers felt a greater amount of points should be awarded at the major superspeedway races than the short tracks.

NASCAR officials said they approved of the way the points system worked and indicated it would likely remain unchanged for several years to come. It remained in place until the 2004 season.

Richard Petty
#43 Dodge
Owner: Petty Enterprises
Sponsor: STP

Starts	30
Wins	13
Top 5	21
Top 10	24
Points	4783
Winnings	$481,750

Fantastic Finish

NASCAR's two most revered icons, Richard Petty and David Pearson, were the primary players in the most stunning finish in NASCAR history. It happened in the Feb. 15, 1976, Daytona 500.

The final 22 laps were a green-flag trophy dash. Pearson held the lead until Petty shot past with 13 laps to go. The pair rode nose-to-tail for 12 laps. Pearson, perched on Petty's rear bumper, was biding his time, content to utilize the draft to slingshot his way into the lead on the final lap.

On the backstretch of the final lap, Pearson gunned his #21 Mercury to the low side and passed Petty to take the lead. Entering the third turn, Pearson hit the banking and drifted up toward the wall, leaving Petty a slight opening in the low groove. Petty pounced on the opportunity and throttled his #43 Dodge alongside Pearson as the pair whipped through the fourth turn.

The cars slapped together and both wobbled. Pearson's car darted nose first into the outside retaining barrier, clipping Petty's rear bumper. Pearson twirled around and slid toward the pit road entrance, clipping Joe Frasson's Chevrolet. Pearson had the presence of

mind to engage the clutch and keep his engine running. Meanwhile, Petty was performing a series of fishtails while trying to keep his car under control, but the car dove into the outside wall.

Petty's car came to a halt on the infield grass less than 100 feet from the finish line. The engine died and Petty frantically tried to restart it. Pearson bumped his car into low gear and inched his way toward the finish line. Driving across the grassy area in the tri-oval, Pearson lumbered past Petty and took the checkered flag at about 20 mph.

Pandemonium ensued as Pearson made his way back around to victory lane. "I'm not sure what happened," said the winner. "He went beneath me and his car broke loose. I got into the wall and came off and hit him. That's what started all the spinning, I think."

After reviewing videotape of the crash, Petty wasn't so sure it was his fault. "You know, I think we were in control when we went through the fourth turn. Then David tapped me and that started all the spinning," he said. "At least me and David did our thing in front of the grandstands so all the people could see it. It must have been quite a finish from their standpoint."

No matter who was to blame, the 1976 Daytona 500 became a classic rubdown between NASCAR's two greatest drivers.

1976
Cale Yarborough

Cale Yarborough broke out of a close points race with Benny Parsons at midseason to score his first NASCAR Cup Series championship. Yarborough won nine races and finished 195 points in front of runner-up Richard Petty.

Yarborough took the points lead for keeps with a 26th-place finish at Talladega in August. Parsons finished 39th after his engine let go in the early laps. Petty passed Parsons in the points race in September and held on for the runner-up spot.

The points lead changed hands eight times among four drivers. Yarborough, Petty, Parsons, and David Pearson traded first place during the early months of the season before it became a three-way battle. David Pearson won 10 races in 22 starts, but finished ninth overall because he ran a limited schedule.

Cale Yarborough
#11 Chevrolet
Owner: Junior Johnson
Sponsor: Holly Farms

Starts	30
Wins	9
Top 5	22
Top 10	23
Points	4644
Winnings	$453,404

1977
NASCAR CUP SERIES CHAMPION
Cale Yarborough

Cale Yarborough was running at the finish in all 30 NASCAR Cup Series races as he dominated the 1977 season to wrap up his second consecutive title. Yarborough won nine races and finished 386 points ahead of runner-up Richard Petty.

Petty captured the points lead briefly at midseason, taking first place after the July 31 race at Pocono. But a runner-up finish the following week at Talladega lifted Yarborough atop the standings again, a lead that he never relinquished.

Benny Parsons finished third in the final standings, winning four races. Six-time winner Darrell Waltrip finished fourth in standings on the strength of six wins. Buddy Baker rounded out the top five, but posted no wins.

Cale Yarborough
#11 Chevrolet
Owner: Junior Johnson
Sponsor: Holly Farms

Starts	30
Wins	9
Top 5	25
Top 10	27
Points	5000
Winnings	$561,641

Allison Wins Daytona 500

Bobby Allison ended a 67-race losing streak with a mild upset win in the Feb. 19, 1978, Daytona 500, outrunning Cale Yarborough and outlasting Buddy Baker in the final laps. Allison suffered through two winless campaigns in 1976 and '77, and accepted an offer from team owner Bud Moore (upper left) in '78 (a ride that Baker had vacated following a disappointing '77 season). Despite crashing in the Twin 125-miler and having to start 33rd in the 500, Allison emerged in a race that featured wrecks and mechanical failures for many contenders.

"I'm so tickled, I can't see straight."
—Bobby Allison

David Pearson's #21 Wood Brothers Mercury battles with
Richard Petty's STP Dodge Magnum in the early stages of the
March 5, 1978, Carolina 500 at Rockingham, N.C.'s North
Carolina Speedway. Temperatures were in the mid 20s at
race time, but Pearson blistered the one-mile track to record

Earnhardt's Lucky Break

Will Cronkrite arranged for young African American road racer Willy T. Ribbs to drive his #96 Cardinal Tractor Co. Ford at Charlotte in May 1978. Ribbs failed to appear for two practice sessions and was arrested in Charlotte for reckless driving. Cronkrite dumped Ribbs and signed 27-year-old Dale Earnhardt to drive his car for a partial season. Earnhardt finished a strong seventh in Daytona's July 4 Firecracker 400 (below), and placed 16th at Darlington's Southern 500 in September (left). Earnhardt made four starts in Cronkrite's car, then caught on with Rod Osterlund for a start in Atlanta's Dixie 500, where he finished an impressive fourth.

Most-Competitive Race

In the Aug. 6, 1978, Talladega 500 at Alabama International Motor Speedway, Lennie Pond drove his #54 Oldsmobile around Benny Parsons with five laps to go, and scored his lone NASCAR Cup Series career victory by a narrow margin. Pond averaged 174.700 mph in the race, a new record. More importantly, when Pond scooted past Parsons down the backstretch, it was the 67th official lead change during the hotly contested 188-lap, 500-mile event. The 67 lead changes established a record in NASCAR Cup Series racing, a mark that would stand for six years. The record finally fell in the May 6, 1984, Winston 500 at Talladega, an event that featured 75 official lead changes. That record still stands today.

1978
Cale Yarborough

Cale Yarborough motored to his record-setting third consecutive NASCAR Cup Series championship in 1978. Yarborough's Junior Johnson team won 10 races and finished a comfortable 474 points ahead of runner-up Bobby Allison. Yarborough clinched the title at Rockingham in October.

Benny Parsons led the points standings from March through June, but Yarborough grabbed the lead with a win at Nashville and never gave it up. Yarborough scored 23 top-five finishes in 30 starts in a near-perfect campaign. Allison won five races, including the Daytona 500.

Darrell Waltrip, a six-time winner, finished third in the standings, while Parsons fell to fourth by the end of the season. Winless Dave Marcis took fifth.

Cale Yarborough
#11 Oldsmobile
Owner: Junior Johnson
Sponsor: Citicorp

Starts	30
Wins	10
Top 5	23
Top 10	24
Points	4841
Winnings	$623,505

Fighting Finish

Number 1 Donnie Allison ran out in front, just ahead of the #11 Oldsmobile of Cale Yarborough in the closing laps of the February 18, 1979, Daytona 500. The two cars tangled down the backstretch on the final lap and clobbered the wall in turn three, knocking both out of the race. Richard Petty, more than a mile behind when the white flag waved, stormed through the accident scene to win his sixth Daytona 500 and end a 45-race winless skid.

After the crash, Cale Yarborough, Donnie Allison, and Bobby Allison engaged in fisticuffs. Bobby had stopped on the track to check on his brother's condition. Cale approached Bobby and punched him as he sat in the car. Bobby dismounted and wrestled with Cale in the infield as Donnie came over to join the free-for-all. The finish and the fight made great television, and helped increase the general public's interest in NASCAR.

1979 Rookie of the Year: Dale Earnhardt

Rookie driver Dale Earnhardt was tabbed to drive the Osterlund Racing Chevrolets and Oldsmobiles in the 1979 NASCAR campaign, and he responded brilliantly. In the April 1 Southeastern 500 at Bristol, Earnhardt edged Bobby Allison and Darrell Waltrip to post his first NASCAR Cup Series victory in only his 16th career start. Earnhardt was leading the July 30 Coca-Cola 500 at Pocono International Raceway when a tire blew, sending him into the boiler-plate retaining wall. Earnhardt broke both collar bones in the accident, and was forced to take six weeks off to recuperate from the painful injuries. David Pearson substituted for Earnhardt until he returned in mid September. Earnhardt finished the season seventh overall on the strength of 17 top-10 finishes.

**Dale Earnhardt
Rookie Record**
#2 Chevrolet, Buick,
Oldsmobile
Owner: Rod Osterlund

Season Rank	7th
Starts	27
Wins	1
Top 5	11
Top 10	17
Points	3749
Winnings	$274,809

1979

NASCAR CUP SERIES CHAMPION

Richard Petty

Richard Petty won an unprecedented seventh NASCAR Cup Series champion-ship thanks to a furious rally late in the 1979 season. Petty trailed Darrell Waltrip by 187 points with just seven races to go. From that point on, Petty never finished lower than sixth.

Waltrip led the points chase most of the season. He assumed command in May, but the lead changed hands in each of the last four races. Waltrip led after the 28th race at North Wilkesboro in October. Petty won at Rockingham the next week and took an eight-point lead. Waltrip finished one spot ahead of Petty at Atlanta, and carried a two-point lead into the season finale at Ontario Motor Speedway in California.

In the final race, Waltrip spun out while trying to avoid another spinning car and lost a lap. Unable to make up the lap, Waltrip finished eighth, while Petty came home fifth and won the title by 11 points.

Richard Petty
#43 Chevrolet, Oldsmobile
Owner: Petty Enterprises
Sponsor: STP

Starts	31
Wins	5
Top 5	23
Top 10	27
Points	4830
Winnings	$561,933

the 1980s ▶▶

The Fabulous Baker Boy

Crew members and well wishers push Buddy Baker's #28 Ranier Racing Oldsmobile into victory lane after his dominating performance in the Feb. 17, 1980, Daytona 500. Baker set an all-time speed record for the Daytona 500, averaging 177.602 mph, a mark that still stands. Baker led 143 of the 200 laps and was comfortably ahead of runner-up Bobby Allison when a late caution flag came out, forcing the race to end under yellow. Baker ended many years of hard luck in The Great American Race; it was his 18th Daytona 500 start. For his efforts, Baker won $102,175, the first time a NASCAR winner took home more than $100,000 in a single event.

A Champion's Last Hurrah

David Pearson, who lost his ride in the Wood Brothers' Mercury in 1979, started his first race of the '80 season in the April 13 Rebel 500 at Darlington Raceway. Driving the #1 Hoss Ellington/Hawaiian Tropic Chevrolet, Pearson started on the front row, bolted to the lead, and was holding down first place when rain curtailed the event five laps after the halfway point. It was the 105th and final career NASCAR Cup Series victory for the three-time champion. Pearson competed in only nine events in 1980 and continued to run a limited schedule through '86.

**DAVID PEARSON
NASCAR
Cup Series
Career Record
1960-1986**
Starts: 574
Wins: 105
Top 5s: 301
Top 10s: 366
Poles: 113
Career Winnings:
$2,836,224

1980
Dale Earnhardt

Dale Earnhardt took the championship points lead in the Daytona 500 and staved off challenges by Richard Petty and Cale Yarborough to capture the 1980 NASCAR Cup Series title. Earnhardt became the first driver to win Rookie of the Year and championship honors in back-to-back seasons.

Petty was within 48 points of Earnhardt in late July, but he broke his neck in a crash at Pocono. Petty concealed the injury from NASCAR so he could continue racing. Relief drivers assisted Petty, but he fell from contention.

Yarborough began his rally in September. He trailed by 173 points following the Richmond event, but then posted a series of top-10 finishes. Going into the season finale at Ontario, Calif., Earnhardt had a narrow 29-point lead.

Earnhardt fell a lap off the pace at Ontario, but muscled his way back onto the lead lap and scrambled to a fifth-place finish. The effort put him 19 points ahead of Yarborough, who took third at Ontario, and gave Earnhardt his first title.

Dale Earnhardt
#2 Chevrolet, Oldsmobile
Owner: Rod Osterlund
Sponsor: Mike Curb
Productions

Starts	31
Wins	5
Top 5	19
Top 10	24
Points	4661
Winnings	$671,990

Downsizing

The Jan. 11, 1981, season opener at Riverside marked the final appearance for full-size cars in NASCAR Cup Series competition. Bobby Allison won the 500-kilometer event in a 1977 Chevy Monte Carlo similar to Darrell Waltrip's #11 car shown below. Until that race, cars as much as five model years old were eligible for NASCAR competition. Effective as of the Feb. 15 Daytona 500, new rules required the use of the newer 110-inch-wheelbase cars vs. the older 115-inch models. Drivers had tested the new cars throughout the winter months and were displeased with the results. "I was nervous as hell in those tests," noted Dale Earnhardt. "These cars aren't stable enough to run in a pack." NASCAR responded by allowing larger spoilers to add stability.

Bobby Allison's Ranier Racing Team brought a sleek 1981 Pontiac LeMans (above) to Daytona, and it proved to have an aerodynamic advantage. Allison had the best car in the race, but finished second to Richard Petty, who prevailed thanks to superior pit stop strategy. Within weeks, NASCAR had enacted new spoiler rules that limited the LeMans more than any other car. Allison switched to Buick (opposite bottom) by May, and no other teams used the LeMans for the rest of the season. Buicks went on to win the first nine races under the new rules, and 22 races for the year. The new smaller Fords (opposite top) won seven races.

Upset at Talladega

Freshman driver Ron Bouchard snookered Darrell Waltrip and Terry Labonte on the final lap of the Aug. 2, 1981, Talladega 500 to provide one of NASCAR's biggest and most spectacular upsets. The veteran Waltrip led entering the final lap, and faded high off the fourth turn to deflect Labonte's charge on the high side. Bouchard, making only his 11th NASCAR Cup Series start, steered his #47 Buick into the open inside lane and won by a bumper in a three-abreast finish with #11 Waltrip and #44 Labonte.

Hollywood Comes to NASCAR

Hollywood director Hal Needham came to NASCAR in 1981 when he launched the Mach 1 Racing Team. Needham originally tabbed Stan Barrett, a land speed record holder, to drive the #33 Skoal Bandit. Barrett made 10 starts for the Mach 1 team, but had difficulty getting acclimated to the heavy NASCAR Cup Series machinery. Barrett posted only one top-10 finish and was replaced by Harry Gant midseason. Gant performed much better and stuck with Needham through 1988, posting nine wins along the way. At the right, Needham (left) poses with (from left to right) Gant, actor Burt Reynolds, and Barrett. Later, Reynolds and Needham teamed up to make the NASCAR-inspired motion picture *Stroker Ace*.

1981
Darrell Waltrip

Darrell Waltrip rallied from a 341-point deficit to bag his first NASCAR Cup Series championship in 1981, as Bobby Allison finished second for the fourth time in his career.

Waltrip was seemingly out of the title hunt in early June, but he began to whittle away at Allison's lead with a series of top-five finishes. With six races to go, Waltrip moved into the points lead with a runner-up finish at Dover. In the final six races, Waltrip extended his lead and finished 53 points ahead of Allison.

Waltrip won 12 races during the 1981 season, while Allison won five times. No one else was close in the points race. Harry Gant finished third, 670 points behind Waltrip, and failed to record a single victory. Terry Labonte and Jody Ridley rounded out the top-five finishers.

Darrell Waltrip
#11 Buick, Chevrolet
Owner: Junior Johnson
Sponsor: Mountain Dew

Starts	31
Wins	12
Top 5	21
Top 10	25
Points	4880
Winnings	$799,134

The Mysterious J.D. Stacy

In 1977, Pennsylvania coal-mining magnate Jim Stacy appeared on the scene, buying the Nord Krauskopf team that had won the 1970 NASCAR Grand National title. Stacy signed driver Neil Bonnett, who managed to win a pair of races.

A little more than a year later, Stacy had no operating capital to keep his team going. Apparently, he had money on paper, but little in his pocket. After Daytona in 1979, Stacy's racing operation shut down amid a flurry of lawsuits.

After a few appearances in 1980, Stacy returned in '81 under the new name J.D. Stacy. He purchased another former championship operation, the Rod Osterlund team that had won the '80 title with Dale Earnhardt. Earnhardt soon quit to join Richard Childress, and Stacy's team scored only a pair of top-five finishes in 19 races.

In 1982, Stacy branched out, sponsoring up to six teams along with his own operation. Predictably, Buddy Baker, Terry Labonte, and Dave Marcis were left holding an empty bag. Tim Richmond won two races for Stacy in '82, but he left to take a more secure driving assignment with Raymond Beadle in '83. Stacy's team floundered in '83, with only four top-five finishes among three drivers.

Stacy once said, "Where I came from, there were only three choices in life—you could coal mine, moonshine, or move-on-down-the-line." By 1984, J.D. Stacy had moved on down the line, never to be actively involved in NASCAR again.

Stroker Ace

Tim Richmond drove the #2 Buick in the May 30, 1982, World 600 at Charlotte Motor Speedway. Richmond's car was decorated with mock sponsorship from Clyde Torkle's Chicken Pit for the 1983 film release *Stroker Ace*. Unfortunately, Richmond crashed early, so little footage of the car in action could be used for the film. The film starred Burt Reynolds, Loni Anderson, Jim Nabors, and Ned Beatty. In the movie, cocky driver Stroker Ace (Reynolds) does everything he can to get out of the promotional contract he unknowingly signed with a greedy fried chicken magnate. Late in the movie, Strocker Ace drove the new 1983 Ford Thunderbird.

1982

Darrell Waltrip

For the second straight season, Darrell Waltrip rallied past Bobby Allison to take the NASCAR Cup Series championship. Driving Buicks for Junior Johnson, Waltrip lagged behind in the points race as Terry Labonte and Allison held the top spots for most of the summer. With four races remaining, Waltrip seized the points lead with an October victory at Martinsville.

For Allison, it was another frustrating end as he finished second in points for the fifth time in his career. Waltrip's win gave team owner Johnson his fifth NASCAR Cup Series championship in the last seven years.

Waltrip won 12 races along the way to his 72-point victory. Allison won eight races. Labonte, who led the points standings most of the way through early August despite failing to record a victory, faded to third place, 278 points behind Waltrip.

Darrell Waltrip
#11 Buick
Owner: Junior Johnson
Sponsor: Mountain Dew

Starts	30
Wins	12
Top 5	17
Top 10	20
Points	4489
Winnings	$923,150

Yarborough Crashes, Wins

Cale Yarborough's #28 Hardee's Chevrolet bounced off the wall and went airborne during qualifications for the Feb. 20 Daytona 500. Yarborough was the first driver to officially top the 200-mph barrier at Daytona, posting a speed of 200.550 mph. It was the quickest time on pole day, but, according to NASCAR rules, the car was withdrawn from the 500, and Yarborough lost the pole position. In the race, Yarborough drove a backup Pontiac that his Ranier Racing team had been using as a show car. Yarborough pushed the Pontiac around Buddy Baker in a frantic last-lap dash to score an unlikely victory.

Petty Differences

Richard Petty labored deep in the field during most of the Oct. 9, 1983, Miller High Life 500 at Charlotte Motor Speedway. In the final laps, however, he bolted past a slew of challengers, including Darrell Waltrip, and went on to win. As Petty celebrated in victory lane, NASCAR officials noticed left-side tires mounted on the right side of his Pontiac, a clear violation of the rules. Further investigation revealed the engine far exceeded the 358-cid maximum. Petty was fined a record $35,000 and docked 104 points for the infractions, but he kept his 198th career NASCAR Cup Series win. The next day, Petty remarked: "It's my job to drive the car. It's is my brother's [Maurice] job to work on the engines. It's his decision as to what to put in the car, not mine." Maurice admitted to cheating, but indicated he did it to keep up with other teams that he felt were bending the rules. King Richard was deeply hurt by the Charlotte fiasco, which became known as "Pettygate." At the end of the season, he left Petty Enterprises to drive for Mike Curb. King Richard returned to his family team in 1986.

1983
Bobby Allison

216

Bobby Allison held off another patented rally by Darrell Waltrip to secure his first NASCAR Cup Series championship in 1983. Allison held a comfortable 170-point lead in late July, but Waltrip shaved the margin down to 41 points by September. Allison responded with three straight wins at Darlington, Richmond, and Dover, and held off Waltrip's last-ditch surge to win by 47 points.

During the course of the season, the points lead changed hands six times among six drivers. In the early weeks of the campaign, Cale Yarborough, Joe Ruttman, Harry Gant, Bill Elliott, and Neil Bonnett traded the lead. Allison took the lead at Dover in May, and held it to the end of the season.

Allison and Waltrip each won six races. Elliott, making his first attempt at the championship, won one race and finished third in the final NASCAR Cup Series points standings.

Bobby Allison
#22 Buick, Chevrolet
Owner: DiGard
Sponsor: Miller High Life

Starts	30
Wins	6
Top 5	18
Top 10	25
Points	4667
Winnings	$883,009

Petty's 200th Win

Richard Petty raced mere inches ahead of Cale Yarborough back to the yellow flag in the final three laps of the July 4, 1984, Firecracker 400 at Daytona International Speedway. Doug Heveron's spin brought out the caution flag, and both Petty and Yarborough were aware that whoever got back to the caution flag first would win the race. Petty prevailed by the width of a bumper to score his much-awaited 200th career NASCAR Cup Series win. President Ronald Reagan witnessed the milestone from the broadcast booth. Motor Racing Network's Ned Jarrett (shown next to the President) interviewed Reagan on MRN's radio broadcast of the race. It marked the first time a sitting U.S. President had attended a NASCAR Cup Series event.

"It's just another number, but it's a big one. I figured I'd eventually get there, but as hard as they've gotten to be, I didn't know when."

—Richard Petty
on his 200th win

1984
NASCAR CUP SERIES CHAMPION
Terry Labonte

Terry Labonte overtook Dale Earnhardt with 10 races to go and held off a late charge by Harry Gant to win the 1984 NASCAR Cup Series championship. Labonte moved into the lead with a victory at Bristol in August.

Gant, who trailed by 131 points in mid August, pulled to within 42 points of Labonte in the season's closing weeks. Labonte ran third in the season finale on the Riverside, Calif., road course to seal his first title by 65 points over Gant.

Labonte won two races, one short track event and one on a road course. He became the first driver since 1973 to win the NASCAR Cup Series title without posting a superspeedway victory.

Bill Elliott won three races and finished third, 131 points behind Labonte. Dale Earnhardt placed fourth with two wins, and Darrell Waltrip, who won a season high seven races, rounded out the top five.

Terry Labonte
#44 Chevrolet
Owner: Billy Hagan
Sponsor: Piedmont Airlines

Starts	30
Wins	2
Top 5	17
Top 10	24
Points	4508
Winnings	$767,715

Dominance Unrewarded

Bill Elliott enjoyed a record-wrecking year in 1985 behind the wheel of the #9 Coors Ford Thunderbird. He won 11 races on superspeedways, an accomplishment still unchallenged in NASCAR's record books. Despite the overwhelming success, Elliott failed to win the NASCAR Cup Series title. A string of mechanical ills and wrecks in the season's last two months opened the door for three-time winner Darrell Waltrip to take advantage of NASCAR's points system and claim his third championship.

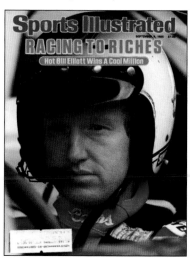

Sports Illustrated
RACING TO RICHES
Hot Bill Elliott Wins A Cool Million

Bill Elliott 1985 Record
#9 Ford
Owner: Harry Melling
Sponsor: Coors

Season Rank	2nd
Starts	28
Wins	11
Top 5	16
Top 10	18
Points	4191
Winnings	$2,433,186

NASCAR's All-Star Race

Beginning in 1985, a special all-star race joined the annual NASCAR Cup Series schedule. The invitational event, called The Winston, was conceived as a nonpoints race, with the previous season's race winners jostling for $500,000 in awards. The inaugural The Winston was held on May 25, 1985, at Charlotte Motor Speedway. Originally, the all-star event was intended to be held at a different track each year. The '86 race took place at Atlanta International Raceway, but a small crowd sent the event back to Charlotte, where it has remained ever since.

Bill France had staged similar races in 1961, '62, and '63 at Daytona, but the '64 event was canceled when only seven teams accepted the invitation to compete.

The Winston of 1985 featured the 12 race winners from '84, and all of them prepared cars to compete in the 105-mile contest. The race was run on Saturday, the day before the World 600. A crowd of 110,000 was on hand.

Darrell Waltrip passed Harry Gant with just over a lap remaining to nail down the first-place prize of $200,000. As Waltrip took the checkered flag, his engine blew to pieces. "Junior [team owner Junior Johnson] said he put a motor in the car that would run 105 miles," said Waltrip. "He had it figured pretty close."

1985
NASCAR CUP SERIES CHAMPION
Darrell Waltrip

The NASCAR Cup Series points system came under fire in 1985 as Bill Elliott, who won a record 11 superspeedway races, was blown away in the points race by three-time winner Darrell Waltrip.

Waltrip, who won the title for the third time, also questioned the points system. "There's not enough incentive for winning the race," said Waltrip. "This year I was the beneficiary of the points system. I've been on the other end of it, too. I will be the first to admit that with the year Bill had, he deserved to be the champion."

Elliott led virtually every category, but lost the championship to Waltrip by 101 points. It was the biggest margin of victory since 1978.

Elliott squandered a 206-point lead in the season's final two months. Waltrip took a commanding lead by finishing 14th at North Wilkesboro in late September as Elliott finished 30th due to transmission problems. Waltrip wasn't threatened during the final four races.

The points lead changed hands 10 times among five drivers. Lake Speed, Terry Labonte, and Geoff Bodine also enjoyed brief stints atop the standings.

Darrell Waltrip
#11 Chevrolet
Owner: Junior Johnson
Sponsor: Budweiser

Starts	28
Wins	3
Top 5	18
Top 10	21
Points	4292
Winnings	$1,318,374

Rookie Kulwicki

Alan Kulwicki's freshman season in NASCAR Cup Series racing was quite remarkable. He bought a Ford Thunderbird race car from team owner Bill Terry in spring, and tackled the NASCAR Cup Series tour with his one-and-only car. Driving the #35 Quincy's Steak House Ford on short tracks, superspeedways, and road courses, Kulwicki managed to log four top-10 finishes. For his determined efforts with a short-handed crew and a single-car operation, Kulwicki was voted 1986 Rookie of the Year.

Alan Kulwicki 1986 Record
#35 Ford
Owner: Alan Kulwicki
Sponsor: Quincy's Steak House

Season Rank	21
Starts	23
Wins	0
Top 5	1
Top 10	4
Points	2705
Winnings	$94,450

Miscalculation

Numerous crashes brought out 120 miles worth of caution flags in the Feb. 16, 1986, Daytona 500, depleting the field. Geoff Bodine and Dale Earnhardt were left to battle it out in the end, but Bodine won easily when Earnhardt, who was running a close second, ran out of gas with three laps to go. The miscalculation was especially bitter for Earnhardt because we was poised to slingshot around Bodine for the win.

1986

Dale Earnhardt

NASCAR changed the name of its top series from Winston Cup Grand National to simply Winston Cup in 1986, and Dale Earnhardt won the first title under the new name. For Earnhardt, it was his second NASCAR Cup Series championship; he finished 288 points ahead of runner-up Darrell Waltrip.

Earnhardt grabbed the points lead in early May with a runner-up finish in Talladega's Winston 500, and never let anybody challenge his healthy advantage for the rest of the season. He held a lead of at least 100 points the entire second half of the season.

Tim Richmond compiled the biggest numbers during the season, winning seven races and eight poles. But a slow start to the season made it impossible for Richmond to overtake Earnhardt. Waltrip won three races and edged Richmond for second place by only six points. Bill Elliott and Ricky Rudd rounded out the season's top five.

Dale Earnhardt
#3 Chevrolet
Owner: Richard Childress
Sponsor: Wrangler Jeans

Starts	29
Wins	5
Top 5	16
Top 10	23
Points	4468
Winnings	$1,768,879

"The Pass in the Grass"

The third annual running of The Winston, NASCAR's all-star race, still ranks as one of stock car racing's most memorable finishes. The three-part event was staged on May 17, 1987, at Charlotte Motor Speedway.

Bill Elliott led virtually all the way in the first two segments. At the start of the final 10-lap dash, Geoff Bodine led going into the first turn. Earnhardt thrust his Chevrolet to the outside, moved beside Elliott, and pinched his Ford rival onto the apron. Elliott's car snagged Bodine's rear bumper as he came back onto the banking. Bodine spun out, carrying Elliott to the high side. Earnhardt bolted to the low groove and took the lead.

For the next few laps, Earnhardt blocked Elliott's attempts to take the lead. Then, Elliott faked to the high side exiting the fourth turn and swept down low. Earnhardt blocked both moves, but fenders made contact. Earnhardt angled across the racing surface and into the grass in the tri-oval. Miraculously, he came back onto the track still in the lead. It was one of racing's most memorable moments, and quickly became known as "The Pass in the Grass," even though no pass was made.

On the back-stretch, Elliott made one final attempt at a pass on the high side. As the pair sped into the turn, Earnhardt guided his car up and nearly forced Elliott into the wall. Two laps later, Elliott blew a tire and fell off the pace. Elliott placed 14th as Earnhardt sped to victory. After the race ended, Elliott weaved his Ford through traffic and popped Earnhardt's rear bumper with a solid lick.

Elliott and Bodine verbally bashed Earnhardt after the race, and all three were all fined and placed on probation by NASCAR. Thankfully, cooler heads prevailed for the rest of the season.

Tragic Figure

After a seven-win season in 1986, the flashy Tim Richmond announced he would be unable to start the '87 season due to double pneumonia. Richmond returned to competitive racing in the May 17 The Winston all-star race, finishing third. He then returned to official NASCAR Cup Series points competition in June and immediately posted back-to-back victories at Pocono and Riverside. Richmond competed in eight races over the next nine weeks before failing health forced him to sit out for the remainder of the year. The Ohio native never raced again and eventually passed away on Aug. 13, 1989.

1987

Dale Earnhardt

Dale Earnhardt blasted out of the starting blocks by winning six of the first eight races in the 1987 NASCAR Cup Series season and coasted to his third championship. By September, Earnhardt had built up a hefty 608-point lead.

On the strength of 11 victories in his 29 starts, Earnhardt finished 489 points in front of runner-up Bill Elliott, who won six races. Earnhardt finished out of the top five in only eight races. The outcome of the championship was never in doubt past April.

Elliott led the standings after the first two races, but Earnhardt claimed the lead with a victory at Richmond on March 8. By the sixth race, Earnhardt held a lead of more than 100 points. He clinched the title after the 27th race of the season at Rockingham.

Besides Earnhardt and Elliott, no other driver won more than two races.

Dale Earnhardt
#3 Chevrolet
Owner: RCR Enterprises
Sponsor: Wrangler Jeans

Starts	29
Wins	11
Top 5	21
Top 10	24
Points	4696
Winnings	$2,069,243

Lap 106

Richard Petty's spectacular crash on the 106th lap of the Feb. 14, 1988, Daytona 500 spewed parts all over the frontstretch at Daytona International Speedway. Petty brushed bumpers with Phil Barkdoll, and was then hit by A. J. Foyt. Petty's Pontiac went airborne and tumbled for a couple hundred yards before being hit by Brett Bodine. The King was shaken up, but not seriously injured in the incident.

Bobby Allison's #12 Buick crossed the finish line two car lengths ahead of runner-up Davey Allison's #28 Ford Thunderbird at the conclusion of the Feb. 14, 1988, Daytona 500. The 1-2 finish by father and son was the first in NASCAR's top division since Lee and Richard Petty ran first and second in a race at Heidelberg, Penn., on July 10, 1960. It marked the 85th and final victory of Bobby Allison's storied career. The Hueytown, Ala., veteran nearly lost his life on June 19 at Pocono. He was airlifted to an area hospital after a first-lap crash and lapsed into a coma. Though he did recover, NASCAR's third all-time-winningest driver never raced again.

1988

Bill Elliott

Bill Elliott overcame challenges by Rusty Wallace and Dale Earnhardt to win the 1988 NASCAR Cup Series title. Wallace led the standings from June to late August, but stumbled in September and was 124 points behind with five races remaining.

Wallace won four of the final five races, but Elliott performed well enough in those events to wrap up his first title. He finished 24 points ahead of Wallace. Earnhardt led the standings from March through early June, but fell off the pace in the season's second half and placed third, 232 points behind Elliott.

For Elliott, the championship was sweet redemption for his bitter defeat in the 1985 NASCAR Cup Series title chase.

Aside from the top three, no other driver seriously contended for the title or won more than two races.

Bill Elliott
#9 Ford
Owner: Melling Racing
Sponsor: Coors

Starts	29
Wins	6
Top 5	15
Top 10	22
Points	4488
Winnings	$1,554,639

Electrifying Finish

The conclusion to the Oct. 15, 1989, Holly Farms 400 at North Wilkesboro Speedway was exciting in more ways than one. Ricky Rudd attempted to duck under Dale Earnhardt's #3 Chevrolet on the last lap. As Rudd pulled his #26 Buick down low, Earnhardt tried to block the move. Rudd had already established position, though, and the two cars collided then spun into the wall. Geoff Bodine seized the opportunity and drove his #5 Levi Garrett Chevy to victory, leading only the final lap. Rudd and Earnhardt finished ninth and 10th, respectively. After the race, the combatants parked on pit road and their crews got together to "discuss" the incident. When interviewed by ESPN, Earnhardt unleashed a profanity-laced barrage, claiming Rudd "should be suspended for the rest of the season." Rudd kept his tongue in check, but didn't mince his words. "I got under him cleanly and he pinched me off and wrecked me. I guess he didn't want to give up the lead."

1989

Rusty Wallace

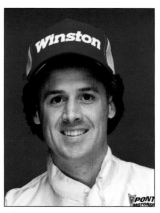

Rusty Wallace took the lead from Dale Earnhardt with five races remaining to win the 1989 NASCAR Cup Series championship.

Wallace and Earnhardt engaged in a hard-fought battle for supremacy during the season. While racing side by side at Rockingham in the 27th race of the 29-race campaign, Wallace slid into Earnhardt, forcing him into a spin. Earnhardt left Rockingham trailing by 109 points, but he staged a furious rally in the final two events.

Needing only to finish 18th in the season finale at Atlanta, Wallace nursed his Pontiac to a 15th-place finish as Earnhardt dominated the race. Wallace squeaked out a narrow 12-point decision over Earnhardt to take his first NASCAR Cup Series title.

Wallace won six times during his championship season, while Earnhardt took five victories. Mark Martin, who scored his first career win at Rockingham, finished third in points, 123 behind Wallace.

Rusty Wallace
#27 Pontiac
Owner: Blue Max Racing
Sponsor: Kodiak

Starts	29
Wins	6
Top 5	13
Top 10	20
Points	4176
Winnings	$2,237,950

the 1990s ▶▶

Days of Thunder

Jerry Bruckheimer and Don Simpson produced *Days of Thunder* for Paramount Pictures. The film starred Tom Cruise as Cole Trickle, a cocky but talented young driver fresh off the Sprint Car circuit. Nicole Kidman costarred as Dr. Claire Lewicki, a neurosurgeon who falls in love with Trickle. Robert Duval played Harry Hogge, a Harry Hyde-like crew chief who has to harness Trickle's talent. Despite several scenes from NASCAR lore (Trickle's crew eating ice cream in the pits, a fender-rubbing rental car duel, Trickle ramming winner Rowdy Burns' car after a race), the movie fell short with most NASCAR fans. The #46 and #51 cars shown were featured in the movie. To get authentic racing scenes from in-car cameras, NASCAR permitted a handful of the movie cars to run a few laps in Daytona's Twin 125-milers and the early laps of the 1990 Daytona 500.

Last-Lap Upset

Number 3 Dale Earnhardt and #10 Derrike Cope race side-by-side in the Feb. 18, 1990, Daytona 500. Earnhardt clearly had the car to beat, leading for 155 of the 200 laps. He was seemingly on his way to an easy victory when a tire blew in the final turn of the final lap, opening the door for Cope to steal his first NASCAR Cup Series victory. Cope's Daytona 500 triumph was also his first career top-five finish.

Disappointing Finish

Mark Martin is consoled by wife Arlene after losing the NASCAR Cup Series championship race to Dale Earnhardt. Martin led the points standings from early June through October, but Earnhardt charged past to capture his fourth championship. Martin actually scored more points than Earnhardt, but the loss of 46 points after his disputed Richmond victory in February proved to be the difference. Martin became only the second driver to lose the title on a penalty. Lee Petty lost the 1950 NASCAR Grand National championship when Bill France docked him 849 points at midseason.

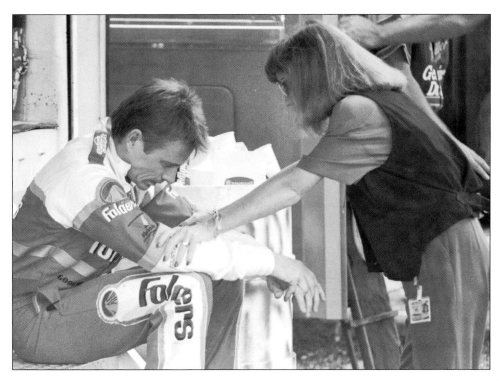

1990
Dale Earnhardt

Dale Earnhardt and Mark Martin battled down to the wire for the 1990 NASCAR Cup Series championship, and Earnhardt nailed down the title in the season's final two races.

Martin led the standings from June through October, but Earnhardt rallied with a win at Phoenix and a third-place effort in the finale at Atlanta. The four-time champion prevailed by 26 points over Martin.

Martin's loss was bitter. Martin won at Richmond in February, but NASCAR officials discovered his carburetor spacer was ½ inch too thick. The team was fined $40,000 and stripped of 46 championship points.

In October, Earnhardt left the pits at Charlotte with the left-side wheels unattached (below), and they flew off in the first turn. His pit crew ran out to the car and put on new tires, ignoring a NASCAR official's command to stay away from the car. Rules state a pit crew can't work on a car when it is on the racing surface. Earnhardt rejoined the race without losing much time. NASCAR considered imposing a penalty, but none was given, and Earnhardt went on to win the title.

Dale Earnhardt
#3 Chevrolet
Owner: Richard Childress
Sponsor: GM Goodwrench

Starts	29
Wins	9
Top 5	18
Top 10	23
Points	44430
Winnings	$3,308,056

Mr. September

Crafty veteran Harry Gant put together a late-season winning streak in 1991 that earned him the nickname "Mr. September." The streak began on Sept. 1 in the 42nd edition of Darlington's Southern 500. Gant pushed his #33 Oldsmobile past Davey Allison's #28 Ford (below) with 70 laps remaining and scampered to a 10-second victory over runner-up Ernie Irvan. With the win, Gant also pocketed a $100,000 bonus from NASCAR title sponsor R. J. Reynolds for winning two of the four events included in the Winston Million promotion. Gant then won at Richmond on Sept. 7 and

Dover on Sept. 15. He posted his fourth straight win on Sept. 22 at Martinsville Speedway (opposite, top), despite getting knocked into the wall in the late stages by Rusty Wallace. Gant sliced through the field following the wreck and nabbed first place from Brett Bodine with 47 laps to go. The veteran from Taylorsville, N.C., appeared to be on his way to his fifth consecutive victory on Sept. 29 in the Tyson Holly Farms 400 at North Wilkesboro Speedway when a malfunctioning O-ring caused a brake failure. The 10-cent part cost Gant $170,000 when Dale Earnhardt passed Gant with nine laps to go (opposite bottom) and drove to victory. Bill Elliott won four straight races in 1992, and Mark Martin did the same in '93.

1991
Dale Earnhardt

Dale Earnhardt claimed his fifth NASCAR Cup Series championship in 1991, finishing comfortably ahead of runner-up Ricky Rudd. Earnhardt won four races along the way to the title and finished 195 points ahead of Rudd in the final point tally.

Earnhardt assumed command of the points race in early May and never trailed again. Rudd managed to cling to second place in the standings despite only one win and nine top-five finishes in the 29-race season.

Ageless Harry Gant provided the most fireworks during the season, winning four races in a row during the month of September. The 51-year-old Gant won five races for the year and had six more top-five finishes than Rudd, but finished a distant fourth in the title race, more than 100 points behind runner-up Rudd.

Davey Allison finished third in the points on the strength of five victories and Ernie Irvan rounded out the top five with two wins.

Dale Earnhardt
#3 Chevrolet
Owner: Richard Childress
Sponsor: GM Goodwrench

Starts	29
Wins	4
Top 5	14
Top 10	21
Points	4287
Winnings	$2,416,685

Instant Classic

The 1992 season finale at Atlanta Motor Speedway became an instant classic. Not only did the Nov. 15 Hooters 500 decide the championship, but two NASCAR heroes crossed paths for the only time in their careers. Seven-time champion Richard Petty started the 1184th and final race of his illustrious 35-year career, while 21-year-old Jeff Gordon made his first NASCAR Cup Series start in the #24 DuPont Chevrolet. Both were involved in accidents and walked away uninjured. Gordon finished 31st and Petty 35th.

The title chase was nothing less than thrilling. Davey Allison needed only to finish fifth in his #28 Ford to wrap up the NASCAR Cup Series championship. Things fell apart when Ernie Irvan spun out on lap 254, blocking Allison's path. Extensive repairs relegated Allison to a 27th-place finish. That left Bill Elliott and Alan Kulwicki to duel for top honors in both the race and the championship chase. Elliott drove his #11 Budweiser Ford to victory as Kulwicki finished second in the #7 Ford "Underbird." Kulwicki and crew chief Paul Andrews calculated the laps led during the race for both warriors, and Kulwicki grabbed the five-point lap-leader bonus when he led the 310th lap. Kulwicki edged Elliott by 10 points to win the title, but the outcome would have been reversed if Elliott had led one more lap. Allison settled for third in the final standings.

1992

NASCAR CUP SERIES CHAMPION

Alan Kulwicki

Alan Kulwicki made a miraculous comeback to win the 1992 NASCAR Cup Series championship by the closest margin in the history of the sport.

Kulwicki trailed Bill Elliott by 278 points with only six races remaining. It was a daunting task to get back into contention, but Elliott's Junior Johnson team ran into a flurry of mechanical problems that allowed several contenders back into the hunt. Elliott led the standings from August through October, but a mechanical failure at Phoenix gave the points lead to Davey Allison going into the season finale.

Allison, who took a 30-point lead into the season-ending Hooters 500 at Atlanta, crashed early, leaving Elliott and Kulwicki to battle it out.

Elliott took the lead with 13 laps to go and won the race. But Kulwicki led the most laps and earned the five-point bonus that goes to the lap leader of each race. Kulwicki edged Elliott by 10 points in the final analysis, and maintaining the lead for a single caution-flag lap was all the difference.

Alan Kulwicki
#7 Ford
Owner: Alan Kulwicki
Sponsor: Hooters

Starts	29
Wins	2
Top 5	11
Top 10	17
Points	4078
Winnings	$2,322,561

The Dale and Dale Show

Dale Earnhardt's string of near misses in the Daytona 500 continued in the Feb. 14, 1993, event. Earnhardt led late in the race, but Dale Jarrett caught Earnhardt at the drop of the white flag and made the decisive pass entering the first turn of the final lap. He was able to stave off Earnhardt the rest of the way and rack up his first Daytona 500 victory. Though bitter for Earnhardt, the moment was made more special by Jarrett's father, Ned, who was calling the race for the CBS Sports live telecast. Ned took over the call on the last lap, rooting his son on to victory. Jarrett's performance also gave team owner Joe Gibbs his first career NASCAR victory. Gibbs, the former Super Bowl-winning coach of the Washington Redskins, had started his NASCAR team the previous year.

Tragedy Off the Track

Tragedy struck twice during the 1993 NASCAR Cup Series season, both times off the track. On April 1, reigning NASCAR Cup Series champion Alan Kulwicki died in a private plane crash en route to Bristol, Tenn., for the Food City 500. On July 12, Davey Allison was gravely injured when the helicopter he was flying crashed on the grounds of Talladega Superspeedway. Allison passed away the following morning. Geoff Bodine bought Kulwicki's team and hired Jimmy Hensley to drive. Allison was replaced by Ernie Irvan in the #28 Robert Yates Ford. Fellow drivers honored their fallen compadres. After the Nov. 10 Hooters 500, Dale Earnhardt and Rusty Wallace carried flags bearing the numbers 28 and 7 in a moving "Polish Victory Lap" tribute. Kulwicki, of Polish heritage, had made the reverse-direction Polish Victory Lap his celebratory signature.

1993
Dale Earnhardt

Dale Earnhardt built a big points lead early in the season and cruised to his sixth NASCAR Cup Series championship in 1993. Earnhardt took the points lead in mid May and paced the standings the rest of the way.

Rusty Wallace trailed by more than 300 points at one point during the season, but then strung together a flurry of wins and top-five finishes, and gradually worked his way back into contention. Wallace won five of the season's last eight races and finished 80 points behind Earnhardt in the final tally.

Earnhardt won six races as Wallace took the checkered flag 10 times. Wallace had more top-five finishes than Earnhardt and an equal number of top-10 finishes, but couldn't overtake his rival in the points chase.

Five-time winner Mark Martin placed third in the final points standings with five wins.

Dale Earnhardt
#3 Chevrolet
Owner: Richard Childress
Sponsor: GM Goodwrench

Starts	30
Wins	6
Top 5	17
Top 10	21
Points	4526
Winnings	$3,353,789

Persistence Pays Off

Sterling Marlin outran Ernie Irvan by two car lengths to post his first career victory in the Feb. 20, 1994, Daytona 500. It was Marlin's 279th career start in 18 years of NASCAR Cup Series competition. After the race, rival pit crews stood at the edge of pit road to congratulate Marlin, who had taken the lead 21 laps from the finish. It was the final win for the Chevrolet Lumina model in NASCAR's biggest annual event. The popular Monte Carlo would return in '95.

A Star is Born

Jeff Gordon, only 22 years old, posted his first two career NASCAR Cup Series victories in 1994. Gordon took the lead from Ricky Rudd with 19 laps to go and sped to his first win in the May 29 Coca-Cola 600 at Charlotte Motor Speedway (middle). On the final round of green-flag pit stops, most of the field took on four tires and fuel. Gordon's crew chief Ray Evernham ordered a two-tire stop. The quick pit stop gave Gordon a lead that he never relinquished. Later, on Aug. 6, Gordon held off Brett Bodine to win the inaugural Brickyard 400 at Indianapolis Motor Speedway (below). More than 340,000 trackside spectators watched Gordon claim his second career victory. With the victory, Gordon served notice he would be a force for years to come.

1994
Dale Earnhardt

Entering the Aug. 21 race at Michigan, Ernie Irvan and Dale Earnhardt were locked in a tight battle for the 1994 NASCAR Cup Series championship. However, Irvan suffered near-fatal injuries in a practice crash before the GM Goodwrench Dealers 400, leaving Earnhardt uncontested for the title.

Earnhardt finished 444 points ahead of runner-up Mark Martin. By claiming his seventh title, Earnhardt tied Richard Petty for the most NASCAR championships. Irvan led the standings after 12 of the first 18 races and appeared to be up to the challenge until his unfortunate crash took him out of the chase.

Earnhardt won four races during the campaign while Martin won twice. Rusty Wallace was again the season's top winner with eight checkered flags, but he finished a distant third in the points. At one point in the season, Wallace won three of five races and never finished below seventh, yet he lost points to Earnhardt during the streak.

Dale Earnhardt
#3 Chevrolet
Owner: Richard Childress
Sponsor: GM Goodwrench

Starts	31
Wins	4
Top 5	20
Top 10	25
Points	4694
Winnings	$3,300,733

NASCAR Trucks

After running four exhibition races starting in July 1994, the NASCAR Super Truck Series made its official debut on Feb. 5, 1995, at Phoenix International Raceway. Mike Skinner won the series' inaugural race, and went on to claim the championship with eight wins and 17 top-five finishes in 20 starts. Skinner won $428,096 for his sterling season. Four pioneering off-road team owners—Dick Landfield, Jimmy Smith, Jim Venable, and Frank Vessels—convinced Bill France, Jr., in 1993 that trucks would be a popular racing attraction. "In only 18 months, this series has risen to a level that took the NASCAR Winston Cup Series 20 years to reach," noted France at the first postseason awards banquet. The series became the NASCAR Craftsman Truck tour in '96, when it acquired backing from Sears' popular tools brand.

Big Shoes to Fill

Bobby Hamilton hooked up with Petty Enterprises in 1995 to drive the famed #43 Pontiac Grand Prix. Hamilton recorded four top-five finishes, including a strong fourth at Martinsville's Goody's 500. The veteran from Nashville has always been regarded as a chassis specialist, and his expertise helped Petty Enterprises improve its on-track performance. Still, the team has never regained the success it enjoyed in the 1960s and '70s.

1995

Jeff Gordon

Young Jeff Gordon took the points lead in the 16th race of the season at Loudon, N.H., in July and held off a gallant rally by Dale Earnhardt to win the 1995 NASCAR Cup Series championship. The 24-year-old Gordon became the second-youngest winner of NASCAR's crown.

With six races remaining, Gordon led Earnhardt by a hefty 309-point margin. With a strong late-season charge, The Intimidator sliced the deficit by large chunks each week. When the checkered flag fell on the season, Earnhardt was only 34 points behind.

Gordon won seven races during his title run. Earnhardt won five events, including two of the final six, as he made a stab to overtake the emerging NASCAR star. Daytona 500 winner Sterling Marlin finished third in the final tally with three victories to his credit.

Jeff Gordon
#24 Chevrolet
Owner: Hendrick Motorsports
Sponsor: DuPont

Starts	31
Wins	7
Top 5	17
Top 10	23
Points	4614
Winnings	$4,347,343

Dale & Dale at Daytona, Part II

Dale Jarrett's #88 Quality Care Ford crossed the finish line two car lengths ahead of runner-up Dale Earnhardt to capture the Feb. 18, 1996, Daytona 500. Jarrett pushed his mount to the front with 24 laps to go and deflected repeated efforts from runner-up Earnhardt to post his second win in NASCAR's most prestigious event. For Earnhardt, it was his third runner-up effort in the last three years. Sterling Marlin's bid to become the first three-time winner of The Great American Race was foiled when his engine blew while he was leading on the 80th lap.

Iron Man

Terry Labonte held off Jeff Gordon's last-lap effort to capture the April 14, 1996, First Union 400 at North Wilkesboro Speedway. The silver paint scheme on Labonte's #5 Kellogg's Chevrolet commemorated his "iron man" streak. By starting the race, Labonte tied Richard Petty's record string of 513 consecutive NASCAR Cup Series starts. Labonte started on the pole and recorded his 17th career victory. Labonte's streak started on Jan. 14, 1979, and continued for 655 races, until it was broken in August 2000. That streak has since been broken by Ricky Rudd, who started his 656th race at Charlotte on May 26, 2002. Rudd's streak continued into the 2004 season with no end in sight.

Winner but not Champion

Since its inception in 1975, NASCAR's points system was criticized for not awarding enough points for a win. It was possible, for instance, for a race winner to earn the same number of points as a second-place finisher if the second-place driver led the most laps. In perhaps no season was this inequity more apparent than 1996. Jeff Gordon won 10 races compared to champion Terry Labonte's two. Gordon also led more laps, and posted the same number of top-five and top-10 finishes. However, Gordon did not finish five races while Labonte didn't finish only three. The difference was enough for Labonte to claim the championship by 37 points over Gordon.

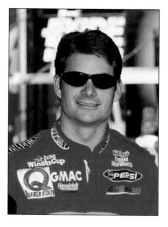

Jeff Gordon 1996 Record
#24 Chevrolet
Owner: Hendrick Motorsports
Sponsor: DuPont

Season Rank	2nd
Starts	31
Wins	10
Top 5	21
Top 10	24
Points	4620
Winnings	$3,428,485

1996

Terry Labonte

Hendrick Motorsports teammates Terry Labonte and Jeff Gordon battled for the 1996 NASCAR Cup Series championship. Labonte parlayed consistency to win his second title 12 years after his first.

Labonte took the lead in the standings with a third-place finish at Rockingham in late October. Top-five finishes in the final two events were enough to capture the title by 37 points over Gordon.

Gordon won 10 races, while Labonte won twice. Both Chevrolet drivers had 21 top-five finishes and 24 top-10 efforts. Gordon led 2314 laps as Labonte led 973 laps. Gordon seemed to have a better year, but Labonte was able to come out on top of the points race thanks to fewer races in which he did not finish.

Four-time winner Dale Jarrett placed fourth in the NASCAR Cup Series standings and two-time winner Dale Earnhardt finished fifth.

Terry Labonte
#5 Chevrolet
Owner: Hendrick Motorsports
Sponsor: Kellogg's

Starts	31
Wins	2
Top 5	21
Top 10	24
Points	4657
Winnings	$4,030,648

Hendrick 1-2-3, Earnhardt Zero

Dale Earnhardt had just been passed by Jeff Gordon for second place on the 189th lap of the Feb. 16, 1997, Daytona 500 when his Goodwrench Chevrolet glanced off the wall. Earnhardt's car tumbled and landed in its wheels. While sitting in the ambulance awaiting a trip to the infield care center, Earnhardt noticed the wheels were still on the car, so he got out of the ambulance and drove the remaining laps to salvage a 31st-place finish. A rash of late-race crashes, Earnhardt's among them, forced the race to end under caution, with Jeff Gordon running first, Terry Labonte second, and Ricky Craven third. The trio crossed the finish line in three-wide formation, giving team owner Rick Hendrick a 1-2-3 finish in The Great American Race. The three stablemates from the Hendrick Motorsports team ganged up on leader Bill Elliott with six laps remaining and made the decisive pass in unison. It was the first time that teammates ran 1-2-3 in NASCAR's biggest event.

Irvan Beats Michigan

Ernie Irvan led the final 20 laps to win the June 17, 1997, Miller 400 at Michigan International Speedway. The victory came three years after a crash at the two-mile superspeedway that nearly took Irvan's life.

Rewind to 1994. Irvan, who had led the points standings for most of the season, was shaking down his Ford in an Aug. 20 practice session. As he sped through the second turn, a tire deflated, sending him into the concrete retaining barrier. The car slid to a halt and medical attendants were on the scene immediately. The quick attention by the Speedway's medical crew helped Irvan survive the first traumatic moments after the crash. Irvan was airlifted to a hospital in Ypsilanti, Mich., in critical condition. He spent months in the hospital recovering from severe head injuries.

Initially, Irvan was given no better than a 10-percent chance of surviving. After 13 months, Irvan returned to NASCAR in late 1995.

Irvan's win laid to rest the ghosts of Michigan past. "I got a little teary-eyed in the last 10 laps," admitted Irvan, "I kept going through turn two thinking, 'Man, this is where the wreck happened.' It started playing with my mind. That wasn't too good, because it's hard to drive with tears in your eyes."

1997
Jeff Gordon

Jeff Gordon prevailed in a three-way showdown with Dale Jarrett and Mark Martin to win the 1997 NASCAR Cup Series championship.

Gordon took the points lead with a September victory in Darlington's Mountain Dew Southern 500, and maintained the narrow advantage over his rivals for the rest of the season. Gordon posted his second NASCAR Cup Series championship by a close 14 points over runner-up Jarrett. Martin was only 29 points behind in the closest three-way title chase in NASCAR Cup Series history.

The points lead changed hands seven times among four drivers. Gordon led most of the season, but Jarrett, Martin, and Terry Labonte enjoyed brief stints atop the points standings.

Gordon racked up 10 wins, including the Winston Million bonus for winning at Daytona, Charlotte, and Darlington. Jarrett won seven events and Martin four.

Jeff Gordon
#24 Chevrolet
Owner: Hendrick Motorsports
Sponsor: DuPont

Starts	32
Wins	10
Top 5	22
Top 10	23
Points	4710
Winnings	$6,375,658

Earnhardt Wins Daytona 500

Dale Earnhardt led a pack of cars down the front chute (left) as they approached the white flag of the Feb. 15, 1998, Daytona 500. Using the lapped car of #75 Rick Mast to prevent Jeremy Mayfield and Bobby Labonte from passing him, Earnhardt won the race back to the caution flag. The final lap was run under caution due to an accident involving John Andretti and Lake Speed. Earnhardt finally prevailed in NASCAR's crown-jewel event after 20 years of trying. He had posted several near misses and had won 32 other races of various types at Daytona, but couldn't take the big one until 1998. The win also halted a career-long 59-race winless streak that stretched back to 1996. After the race, Earnhardt was congratulated by a reception line that included crews of virtually every other team. "To see all those guys come out [on pit road] was pretty impressive," said Earnhardt, who led the final 61 laps. Earnhardt earned $1,059,805 for the win.

Dale Earnhardt's Record at Daytona		
	Cup Series	Twin 125s
Starts	46	23
Top 5	22	18
Top 10	34	20
Wins	3	12*

* Includes 10 in a row from 1990 to 1999

* Earnhardt also won 7 Late Model Sportsman and NASCAR Busch Series races, 6 Busch Clash and Budweiser Shootout events, and 6 IROC races at Daytona International Speedway for a total of 34 wins

1998

Jeff Gordon

Jeff Gordon moved past Jeremy Mayfield in late June to take the NASCAR Cup Series points lead and left all rivals to battle over the leftovers. Gordon motored to a 364-point win to capture his third title during NASCAR's 50th anniversary season.

Gordon won 13 races, tying a modern-era mark established by Richard Petty in 1975. Mark Martin finished a distant second to Gordon, marking his third runner-up finish.

Over the course of the season, the points lead changed hands five times among four drivers. Rusty Wallace, Dale Earnhardt, and Mayfield traded the lead before Gordon assumed command.

Third-place finisher Dale Jarrett won three races, but his title hopes were dashed with poor finishes at Martinsville and Charlotte in the fall.

Jeff Gordon
#24 Chevrolet
Owner: Hendrick Motorsports
Sponsor: DuPont

Starts	33
Wins	13
Top 5	26
Top 10	28
Points	5328
Winnings	$9,306,584

Busy Rookie Season

Tony Stewart's rookie season in 1999 was one of the most eventful in the history of NASCAR Cup Series racing. The 27-year-old from Rushville, Ind., finished fourth overall in the championship chase on the strength of three wins (all in the season's second half), 12 top-five finishes, and 21 top-10 showings. On May 30, he raced in two events on the same day, finishing ninth in the Indy Racing League's Indianapolis 500 (inset) and fourth in NASCAR's Coca-Cola 600 at Charlotte Motor Speedway. The cocky rookie made headlines of a different kind on Oct. 3 at Martinsville Speedway. Stewart and Kenny Irwin, Jr., tangled three times during the race, and Stewart spun out after the third altercation. After exiting his car, Stewart threw his heel pads at Irwin and tried to climb inside the rolling #28 Ford to further "discuss" the incident (opposite, bottom). The emotional outburst would be the first of many for the rising stock car star.

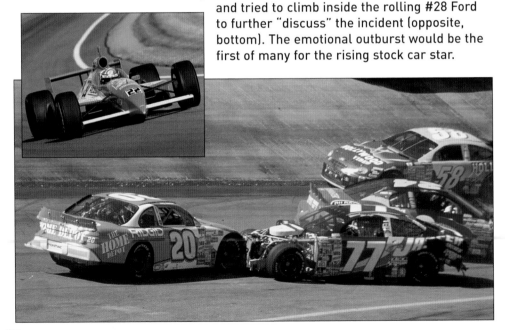

1999

Dale Jarrett

Dale Jarrett moved into the NASCAR Cup Series points lead in May with a victory at Richmond and never gave a backward glance as he stormed to his first championship. Jarrett won four races during the 34-race campaign and finished 201 points ahead of runner-up Bobby Labonte.

Jarrett became the second second-generation driver to reach the pinnacle of stock car racing. He and his father Ned joined Lee and Richard Petty as the only father-son combinations to wear the championship crown.

Labonte won five races en route to the runner-up spot in the title chase. Two-time winner Mark Martin came in third. Jeff Gordon won the most races, with seven, but finished sixth.

Jarrett gave owner Robert Yates his first NASCAR Cup Series championship.

Dale Jarrett
#88 Ford
Owner: Robert Yates
Sponsor: Ford Quality Care

Starts	34
Wins	4
Top 5	24
Top 10	29
Points	5262
Winnings	$6,649,596

the 2000s ▶▶▶

First & Last for Father & Son

The 2000 season proved historic for NASCAR and the Earnhardt family. Flashy rookie Dale Earnhardt, Jr., drove away from all challengers down the stretch in the April 2 DirecTV 500 at Texas Motor Speedway to post his first career victory. It was only the younger Earnhardt's 12th NASCAR Cup Series start. Later that year, Dale, Sr., won the Oct. 15 Winston 500 at Talladega Superspeedway. Earnhardt put on a monumental rally in the last five laps, charging from 18th place to first. It was Earnhardt's 76th and final NASCAR Cup Series win; the NASCAR superstar would tragically die after a crash at the 2001 Daytona 500.

2000

Bobby Labonte

Bobby Labonte gave team owner Joe Gibbs his first NASCAR Cup Series championship to go with the former Washington Redskins coach's three Super Bowl rings in 2000. Labonte took the points lead with a runner-up finish at California Speedway in April and held on to record his first career championship.

Labonte posted four victories and held off a mild late-season rally by Dale Earnhardt to win the title by 265 points. Earnhardt won twice, including a dramatic win at Talladega in October when he came from 18th place to first in the final five laps.

Four-time race winner Jeff Burton finished third in the NASCAR Cup Series standings, 29 points behind Earnhardt. Super sophomore Tony Stewart racked up the most wins with six, including the first of his career, and finished sixth in the championship points race.

Bobby Labonte
#18 Pontiac
Owner: Joe Gibbs
Sponsor: Interstate Batteries

Starts	34
Wins	4
Top 5	19
Top 10	24
Points	5130
Winnings	$7,361,386

Dodge Returns to NASCAR

The Dodge division of Chrysler Corp. returned to NASCAR Cup Series racing for the first time since the late 1970s, assembling a formidable team for the 2001 season. Ray Evernham, who left the Hendrick Motorsports Chevrolet operation in '99, was hired by MoPar to direct Dodge's effort. Evernham was in charge of Dodge's two-car flagship team with drivers Casey Atwood (#19) and Bill Elliott (#9). Other Dodge teams included Bill Davis Racing, Felix Sabates, Melling Racing, and Petty Enterprises, which returned to the Chrysler fold for the first time since '78. Dodge won four races in 2001, with #40 Sterling Marlin taking the first at Michigan in August. Elliott won at Homestead (below) to post his 41st career victory.

Evernham Motorsports
2001 NASCAR Winston Cup Series

Dodge Different.

Tragedy at Daytona

On the final lap of the Feb. 18, 2001, Daytona 500, Dale Earnhardt, Sr., squeezed a tad low while battling Sterling Marlin for third place. The cars touched and Earnhardt's Chevrolet clobbered the wall nearly head-on. Dale Earnhardt, Inc. drivers Michael Waltrip and Dale Earnhardt, Jr., bolted under the checkered flag as the elder Earnhardt's skidding car came to a halt inside the fourth turn. Emergency workers cut the top off Earnhardt's car and administered to the stricken driver. He was transported to the hospital and pronounced dead at 5:16 P.M. The official announcement came nearly two hours later when NASCAR president Mike Helton, who had taken over the position in the off-season, uttered the words nobody wanted to hear: "Today . . . we lost Dale Earnhardt."

The NASCAR community paid its respects to its fallen icon throughout the rest of the season. Telecasts honored Earnhardt with a silent third lap, and pit crews and fans mourned openly. Rookie Kevin Harvick, Earnhardt's replacement, won in just his third start, then drove around the track in reverse direction showing three fingers in honor of the fallen Dale Earnhardt.

New Tracks, New Markets

In 1997, new racetracks opened in Texas and California, bringing NASCAR Cup Series racing back to markets that hadn't hosted races since the 1980s. Two more tracks opened in 2001, this time welcoming NASCAR to areas of the country that hadn't had it before. The new Chicagoland Speedway, located in Joliet, Ill., hosted the inaugural Tropicana 400 on July 15 (below). Todd Bodine won the first pole, and rookie Kevin Harvick drove his #29 Chevrolet to victory (opposite, top). The new Kansas Speedway (opposite bottom and right) hosted its first NASCAR Cup Series race on Sept. 30. The Protection One 400 attracted a wall-to-wall crowd who watched Jason Leffler claim the pole position and Jeff Gordon motor to his sixth win of the season. Gordon's win put him 222 points ahead of Ricky Rudd, leaving him in prime position to capture his fourth championship.

2001
NASCAR CUP SERIES CHAMPION
Jeff Gordon

Jeff Gordon took the NASCAR Cup Series points lead with an eighth-place finish at Pocono in July, then romped to his fourth championship with ease. After being locked in a tight battle during the first half of the season, Gordon left all challengers in the dust as he won by a 349-point cushion over runner-up Tony Stewart.

The points lead changed hands seven times among five different drivers early in the year. By late summer, it was a one-horse race with Gordon leading by more than 300 points in August.

Gordon won six races along the way to his fourth title. Stewart overcame a sluggish start to finish second on the strength of three victories. Two-time winner Sterling Marlin finished third in the points chase with two wins. Ricky Rudd and Dale Jarrett rounded out the top five. Jarrett posted the second-most wins of the season with four.

Jeff Gordon
#24 Chevrolet
Owner: Rick Hendrick
Sponsor: DuPont

Starts	36
Wins	6
Top 5	18
Top 10	24
Points	5112
Winnings	$10,879,757

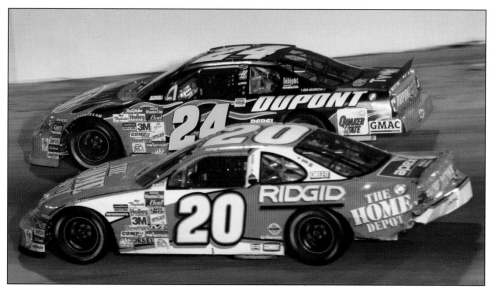

Marlin's Gaff, Burton's Win

During a red flag five laps from the finish of the Feb. 17, 2002, Daytona 500, Sterling Marlin climbed from his #40 Dodge on the backstretch and pulled a bent fender away from his right front tire. Marlin, who was leading at the time, had crumpled the fender in a skirmish with Jeff Gordon. NASCAR rules prohibit any work from being done to a car during a red flag, and Marlin was flagged to the pits when the race con-

tinued. Marlin resumed the chase in 14th place, but battled back to finish eighth. Ward Burton, who took the lead for the first time with five laps remaining, wheeled his #22 Dodge to a narrow victory over Elliott Sadler. Burton gave Dodge its first win in The Great American Race since 1974.

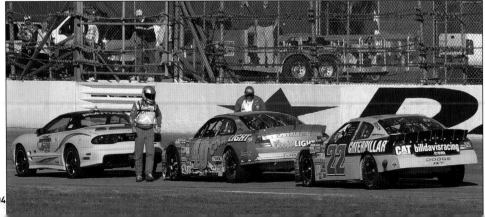

DEI Dominance

Dale Earnhardt, Jr., won both races at Talladega Super-speedway in 2002, while his Dale Earnhardt, Inc. (DEI) teammate Michael Waltrip won one of two at Daytona. The performances extended a string of DEI-car dominance at NASCAR's grandest super-speedways. In 2001 and '02, the DEI cars of Earnhardt and Waltrip won six out of eight races at Talladega and Daytona. The streak extended into 2003 as well, when the DEI cars won three of four at NASCAR's biggest tracks.

Young Guns

Darrell Waltrip once said "old age and treachery" would win out against "youthful exuberance" in most instances. In 2002, that time-honored assessment no longer rang true. The '02 season saw a new wave of NASCAR drivers, the "young

Matt Kenseth

guns," take the sport by storm. Kurt Busch, Dale Earnhardt, Jr., Kevin Harvick, Jimmie Johnson, Matt Kenseth, Jamie McMurray, Ryan Newman, and Tony Stewart—all with less than five years experience—combined to win 20 of the 36 NASCAR Cup Series races, and Stewart captured the championship. Busch won three of the final five races and finished third in points. Rookies Johnson and Newman placed fifth and sixth, respectively. Kenseth won the most races and finished eighth in the standings. Earnhardt, Jr., won both Talladega races, and

Ryan Newman

Harvick won at Chicago. McMurray's win at Charlotte was historic because it came in only his second career NASCAR Cup Series start. In 2002, the young guns showed the old dogs that youthful enthusiasm sometimes trumps experience.

Kevin Harvick

Jimmie Johnson (#48) and Kurt Busch (#97)

Kurt Busch

Dale Earnhardt, Jr.

Jamie McMurray

2002
Tony Stewart

Bad-boy Tony Stewart rallied from a last-place finish in the season-opening Daytona 500, scrambled back into contention, and delivered a late-season kick to capture the 2002 NASCAR Cup Series championship.

Stewart took the lead in the points standings with a runner-up finish at Talladega in the 30th event of the 36-race campaign. Rookie Jimmie Johnson led going into the Talladega event, becoming the first rookie to lead the NASCAR standings since Dick Hutcherson in 1965.

Sterling Marlin led the points race from February through late September, but his season ended when he injured his neck at Kansas Speedway. Mark Martin, Johnson, and Stewart all led the standings in the final stretch.

Stewart cruised to an 18th-place finish in the season finale at Homestead-Miami Speedway to seal his first title. He finished 38 points ahead of runner-up Martin, who finished second in the NASCAR Cup Series points chase for the fourth time in his career.

Tony Stewart
#20 Pontiac
Owner: Joe Gibbs
Sponsor: Home Depot

Starts	36
Wins	3
Top 5	15
Top 10	21
Points	4800
Winnings	$9,163,761

Winnin' in the Rain

Michael Waltrip dashed around leader Jimmie Johnson on the 106th lap of the Feb. 16, 2003, Daytona 500. Waltrip was still leading when the second downpour of the day halted NASCAR's most-celebrated event after 109 of 200 laps had been completed. Waltrip's DEI Chevrolet was only in the lead for about three minutes on the track, but his #15 sat atop the scoreboard for nearly two hours in the rain before NASCAR was forced to call the race official. Waltrip's celebration didn't come from behind the wheel, but from a damp pit lane when the announcement was made.

Safety Hatch

Michael Waltrip pops through the roof of his #15
Chevrolet after a dramatic win in Talladega's EA Sports
500 on Oct. 28. Waltrip staved off a last-lap challenge
from Dale Earnhardt, Jr., to score his second win of the
season. Waltrip's Dale Earnhardt Inc. team was among
the first to experiment with the roof hatch as an emergency escape device late in the 2003 season.

Darlington Duel

With smoke trailing behind them, #32 Ricky Craven and Kurt Busch ground toward the finish line in the thrilling conclusion to the March 16, 2003, Carolina Dodge Dealers 400 at Darlington Raceway. Craven nipped Busch by 0.002 second, the closest finish in NASCAR Cup Series history. Craven's triumph was the only one for the Pontiac nameplate in 2003 and may be its last win in NASCAR's top level of competition. In October, Pontiac announced it was withdrawing from NASCAR.

NASCAR's New Direction

Major changes took place in 2003 that would affect NASCAR's future. On June 19, NASCAR announced Nextel Communications would become the title sponsor of its top racing series in 2004, changing its name from NASCAR Winston Cup to NASCAR NEXTEL Cup. Then, on Sept. 13, Bill France, Jr., stepped down as NASCAR's chairman and chief executive officer and named his 41-year-old son Brian (left) as his successor. In December, reports surfaced indicating NASCAR would adopt a new points procedure to determine the 2004 NASCAR NEXTEL Cup champion. An increased number of points would be awarded to race winners, and a 10-race NASCAR NEXTEL Chase for the Cup would make up the final portion of the season. The top 10 in the points standings after the 26th race would qualify for the final 10-race chase.

All or Nothing

Ryan Newman put together an impressive, though disappointing, season in 2003. The 25-year-old driver from South Bend, Ind., won eight races in just his second full season in NASCAR Cup Series racing. Though he led all drivers in wins, it wasn't enough for Newman to challenge for the NASCAR Cup Series Championship. Crashes at Daytona, Talladega, and Bristol contributed to an eighth-place overall finish in the points race. Consistency helped Matt Kenseth win the title despite just one win. The seeming inequity between Kenseth and Newman was one factor in NASCAR's decision to change its points system after the 2003 season.

**Ryan Newman
2003 Record**
#12 Dodge
Owner: Roger Penske
Sponsor: Alltel

Season Rank	6th
Starts	36
Wins	8
Top 5	17
Top 10	22
Points	4711
Winnings	$6,100,877

2003
Matt Kenseth

Matt Kenseth dominated the 2003 season with consistency. The Cambridge, Wisc., native only won one race but held the points lead for most of the year. With a fourth-place finish in the March 9 Bass Pro Shops MBNA 500 at Atlanta, Kenseth moved atop the points standings and never trailed again. He had only two DNFs the entire year.

Kenseth coasted home 90 points in front of runner-up Jimmie Johnson, and became the fourth driver to capture the title with only one win.

Kenseth led the points after 33 of the 36 races, the most dominating performance since Dale Earnhardt led after all but two races in 1987. He also led the points standings more than any driver since Richard Petty led after 41 of 48 races in '71.

Kenseth, who gave owner Jack Roush his first title, was also the final champion crowned by series sponsor Winston. In 2004, Nextel Communications became the title sponsor for NASCAR's top racing series.

Matt Kenseth
#17 Ford
Owner: Jack Roush
Sponsor: DeWalt

Starts	36
Wins	1
Top 5	11
Top 10	25
Points	5022
Winnings	$9,422,764

1952...